Only on Sundays

Only on Sundays

KATHARINE WHITEHORN

METHUEN & CO LTD

11 NEW FETTER LANE · LONDON EC4

First published in 1966
© *The Observer 1963, 1964, 1965, 1966*
© *Punch 1960, 1963*
Printed in Great Britain by
Latimer Trend & Co Ltd Plymouth

To

George Seddon

my wise and kindly boss
who got me on to the *Observer* in the first place, and
has since protected what I wrote from all possible
attacks by printers, advertisers, management, lawyers,
common sense and People Who Knew Better. In his
early days he used to boast of being the only man
on the *Manchester Guardian* who could milk a cow;
he can still cope with women journalists better than
anyone else in Fleet Street.

Acknowledgments

Only on Sundays is only partly true. It has to be admitted that two of these pieces (Just You Wait, 'Enery 'Iggins and In Defence of Excess) came out on a Wednesday—in *Punch*. I am indebted to its Editor for kindly allowing me to reprint them here.

My thanks are also due to the editor of the *Observer*, in which the rest of these articles first appeared.

K. W.

Contents

7

1 · *Aunt for Aunt's Sake*

Christmas approaches, the time of string bags and tinsel, carols and gastric flu; but also, pre-eminently, the time for aunts. And the annual question presents itself: Are aunts declining?

It is all very well for Bertie Wooster to say that in this life it is not aunts that matter but the courage one brings to them: far more important is the question of whether aunts, in the richest sense of the word, may not be dying out.

If so, it will be a bad day for literature: for few words imply so much of what they don't actually mean as the word 'aunt'. Indeed, when you think of the unbridled individuality of real aunts it is amazing that *The Times* and the BBC should flinch at being called Auntie; it is a name, one would have thought, of which they could make a hammer to crush and astound their critics.

Learning, as from Pope, that true ease in writing comes from aunt, not chance, I have often dragged my own aunts into articles, and such is the astonishing profusion and variety of these ladies that features editors have frequently accused me of making them up – which only goes to show that features editors are crazy, as one obviously couldn't.

Aunts whose benign (and indeed only) legacy has been their anecdotal value include Great-Aunt Mabel, a pioneer of plus-fours for women, who bicycled furiously over the lumpier moors of Scotland with two cairn terriers in her bicycle basket; Great-Aunt Gertie, who would sing *Where My Caravan Has Rested* off-key after dinner, and Great-Aunt Carrie who sang *chords* ('In my time I have sung soprano, alto, tenor and bass; and now—I sing them all. My dear, I sing chords.').

There was my mother's Aunt Gracie, who mortified her as a child by letting down all her (my mother's) knickers so that they showed beneath her dresses: Aunt Connie, who had no stomach, and Great-Aunt Ursula, who has an O.B.E. and an aluminium hip.

There was the pick of the bunch, Great-Aunt Marion, who took a double first at Edinburgh University when she was over forty and went to Paris to study art when she was seventy, so that much of her best work was done through binoculars with the fading eyes of old age; she died because though there were only two other elderly ladies in the house, she always locked her bedroom door before undressing, and fell down and broke a leg behind it.

My husband and I each have one corker of an aunt, his being a splendid misanthropist whose considered view of life is 'Don't like dogs. Don't like cats. Don't like people much.' The one thing we have lacked is a really wicked aunt: it would have been nice to have one who drank, or turned a missionary settlement into a nudist colony, or ran away to sea. I did have one who came home once with a black eye and announced she had knocked down a soldier in the High Street; but this turned out, as usual, to be but the effects of erratic bicycling.

It is sometimes argued that it is the numerical decline of spinsters which may cause a decline in aunts; but I doubt if this has anything to do with it. Many of the above nuts had accompanying if unmemorable uncles; so had P. G. Wodehouse's terrifying Aunt Agatha, who ate broken bottles and wore barbed wire next to the skin; so had the Thurber aunt who thought that electricity leaked unseen from every unplugged light socket; so had Bernard Levin's Aunt Lilian, who, though actually keeping a shop selling classy underwear, became the possessor of some hundreds of terra-cotta masks of Montgomery, which can hardly have been of much interest to those wishing to buy petticoats and stockings, or, indeed, to anyone else except possibly Monty himself. She was also the one who sent a Christmas Card to the Rabbi.

But it is true that things which are distressing in a mother merely add to the richness of the mixture in an aunt. All this chat goes on about whether it is as wife, mother or assistant office manager that Woman really fulfils herself: but obviously it is as aunt that her personality really stretches to the full.

I think, too, that people who believe aunts are on the decline do not sufficiently allow for the time factor: for if women burgeon marvellously as aunts, it is as great-aunts that they come into their most riotous flower.

This is why it takes such an extraordinarily long time for smart Christian names to come into vogue again: they have to wait till all memory of the great-aunts has died out. All the little Harriets and Emmas and Charlottes in their prams today bear *early*-nineteenth-century names; it will be some time yet before we have a similar revival of Muriels and Maisies and Violets; and as for the Pats and Jills and Pams of the thirties – though technically aunts already – why, they have hardly begun.

Every family needs a complete set of aunts, adopted if necessary. There should be one splendid aunt, to act as an outrigger for the parents, as it were: her point of view sanctioned by common ancestry but uncomplicated by all the tensions so apt to occur between parents and teenagers. There should be one perfectly awful aunt, to unite the said parents and teenagers in opposition – witness the Durrell family on Corfu, moving an entire household of mother, three sons, daughter, dogs and an uncounted number of gulls, toads and geckoes into a smaller house simply in order to avoid the visit of Great-Aunt Hermione, 'that evil old camel, smelling of mothballs and singing hymns in the lavatory'.

There should be one thoroughly subversive aunt, to cast doubt – but still doubt authorized by ties of blood – on all the principles the parents hold most dear (I had this frivolous blonde aunt, who set me up at fourteen with a pair of silk cami-knickers and a rolled gold bangle). And there can be any number of rich, kind or merely eccentric aunts to serve as material for stories, food for thought or merely Horrible Warnings.

It has just dawned on me in a blinding flash that I *am* an aunt, albeit of nephews as yet hardly off the horizontal. What golden opportunities stretch ahead! What magnificent possibilities! Only time will show, I suppose, into which category I shall fall; I just hope I do not go down in family history as the aunt who was gunned down by her own aunts, for failure to pay them due respect.

2 · Never Mind Why It Hurts

Medical fights are not usually ones in which anybody can join in: the slashing of scalpels draws too much blood. But the effect of a medical theory on public opinion is another matter; and I think we have a right to be worried about the general effect of the 'Tell doctor *why* it hurts' school of medicine.

I once worked for an editor who believed in psychosomatic medicine. If I rang him up and said I was feeling too ill to write he would say, not 'What have you got?' but 'What are you trying to evade?' and he would no doubt have attributed the high incidence of bouncing good health among his staff to his skill in keeping these little woolly creatures happy.

He had a collector's interest in a good many forms of fringe medicine: 'Just think!' he would say. 'I've found a man who practises hypnotism *and* acupuncture!' (His only comment on the Ward case has been 'This will set the cause of osteopathy back ten years.') The main reason he felt that odd treatments might be effective was that they worked on the mind of the patient; and in the mind of the patient, he thought, all illness began. He left us all finally convinced of the importance of psychosomatic medicine; but I personally ended up equally certain that if ever there was a drug that should be taken only under the strictest medical supervision, psychosomatic medicine was it.

People who know about psychosomatic medicine tell you till they are blue in the face (a well-known stress symptom) that psychosomatic illnesses are simply those in whose origin the mind plays a part. They are just as real as any others; the measles are as spotty, infectious and revolting if some slight part of the subconscious let down the drawbridge to them as if they swarmed the body's battlements unaided.

'Hysterical' ailments, where the mind acts directly on the body – for example when it paralyses a hand to prevent its writing an examination – are quite different (though even those, it might be noted, are something the conscious mind cannot control). So to suggest that the patient 'snap out of it' and cure himself, just because psychological misery may have helped him get ill, is about as sensible as suggesting that if a man throws himself off a cliff for unrequited love, the voice of his beloved yelling 'I love you' from above will cause him to stop in mid-air and rise back up again.

There are, in any case, plenty of objections to be made to too sweeping a theory of psychosomatic medicine. Even the most rudimentary acquaintance with cars and refrigerators and electricity suggests that at least some of our mortal ills must be due to simple mechanical failure: there is always sheer accident – things like car crashes and epidemics; and the speed with which an animal responds to an injection even in circumstances which (judging by the scratches down my left arm) must be highly traumatic shows there must be *something* in the syringe that works.

But while the medicine men are still undecided on the matter, a good many ordinary people have adopted the theory with disquieting speed. It is not just that the medical advance is attended by a certain amount of lay confusion: confusion and the lay mind go together like witches and newts' blood. What is alarming is the way people attribute illness to mental causes – if doing so will let them off being sympathetic.

One of my relations got a disagreeable new job and a new depressive illness at about the same time: we all rather patronizingly assumed that all he had to do was change the job. And so he did – a couple of years later; but it was a good strong drug that cured the depression in a matter of weeks.

14

I know a woman in her forties whose one grief is her child-lessness; her friends have given up being sympathetic, opting instead for the easier idea that of course, she didn't really *want* children. And I have heard the same said of single women – 'psychologically unsuited' is the phrase used – even of the generation that lost a million eligible men to the war.

An old woman's arthritis may be the one thing that brings her sympathy and visitors. But the same causes that make her, mentally, a crotchety old party may be seizing up her joints physically; to suggest that she is 'doing it all on purpose' simply lets us off being sympathetic.

There seems to be a new indifference about, a new Candi-deism: we need not really worry about other people's troubles because they are supposed to be fulfilling the secret wishes of the people concerned. The basis for sympathizing with some-one's illness seems to be the conviction that they cannot help it; misunderstanding psychosomatic medicine makes us think that people can help it, and the result can be an astonishing hard-heartedness. But in fact any illness that may be caused by stress needs not less sympathy, but a double lot; one for the illness, and one for the misery that helped to cause it.

We have become more humane about mental illness since we have treated it as physical: no one now laughs at a cretin. But we are in danger of becoming less humane about physical illness by regarding it as mental. While the body's troubles are the only ones our sympathies know how to embrace, we had better not be in too much of a hurry to believe that they are all in the mind.

3 · *The Simple Life*

Balmain tells a story of an American magazine editress being visited in her cabin on her way home from Paris. She had ten chains round her neck and fourteen on her wrist and three rings on each hand; her throat was a mass of ruffled silk and the jacket of her crimson suit was interlined and pocketed with the same material: she had bows on her two-tone shoes. '*Do* tell me,' said her friend, 'what's the fashion in Paris.' And the editress lifted her bejewelled hand in the air and said: 'Simplicity!'

Illusions of simplicity are one of the big fevers of civilization and they break out worse in the hot weather than any other time. It is in August that people dream of getting away from All This, from the world of anger and telegrams, stockings and cars and insurance payments, and leading the Simple Life.

We have recently been to stay with some friends who are lucky enough actually to be leading the simple life, having retired to a remote village to write novels. They would explain how their minds were no longer clogged with worrying about publishers' intrigues and take-over bids, and what *was* all this about Προφύμω anyway? And they would then plunge into a passionate description of a village row, involving the mayor, two policemen, a nymphomaniac and six dogs of which one was mad. The row involved the passionate intrigue of everyone for miles around, providing one more demonstration that any village worth its salt can set up a web of intrigue that makes sixteenth-century Venice seem like a game of snap.

There was also the domestic simplicity. They would say how much easier it was for them not to have a telephone – though people who tried to ring them had to wait twenty-four hours for them to be traced, approached by a messenger boy and asked to ring back from the Post Office. The husband said how much easier it was to walk down the hill to the village than to drive into London. His wife, who was walking up the hill thwacking the donkey, was too out of breath to say anything.

She spent her days bent like a croquet hoop cleaning pitted stone floors with a hand broom, and they heated the water for washing up in a bucket over a charcoal stove, and it all took a lot of time. I could not help being reminded of a friend who went firewatching in the Canadian backwoods so that he could discover the meaning of the universe: he spent so much time carting wood and drawing water he never even discovered the meaning of the *Fire Watchers' Manual*.

Probably the simplest life anyone ever led was St Simeon Stylites on the top of his pillar – rivalled only by a cat I read about who lived for nine years at the top of a tree in Brazil. She was fed by people who respected her desire for privacy, which was not, however, as complete as St Simeon's: several litters of kittens dropping to the ground suggested that she enjoyed an adequate social life. These two certainly lived simply – but they could hardly have done so for more than a day or two if they had not suckered other people into collecting food, paying for it and manoeuvring it up to them.

The cat and St Simeon thus proved they had grasped the essential point which my simple-lifing friends seem to me to have missed: that simplicity consists in getting bothersome irrelevancies out of the way, and that therefore the best place to be simple is at the top of a pyramid of other people's exertions. The simplest way to get fed is not to start by grinding your own corn; it is to be in an hotel room and pick up a telephone and order a meal cooked by someone else to be sent up.

The simplest way to starch a collar is not to boil rice, and soak your collar in the stuff that comes off the top; and get it to the right state of wetness and then iron it; it is to pick up an aerosol can and simply spray the starch on; and the hideous expense of the thing testifies to the complication that went into making the can.

The simpler the raw materials of life are, the more complicated a time you have making them usable. An utterly simple dress of the couture sort, where even the seams hardly show, takes centuries of sophistication, tremendous traditions of textile manufacture, all the neuroses of the designer and the military disciplines of the workrooms to produce: a savage or a peasant would just make do with elaborate embroidery or intricate decorations of shark's teeth. Simplicity, for the consumer, is the fine flower of civilization – a fact which becomes particularly apparent when civilization breaks down. Last winter we *all* became simple villagers: we lived in one room because there was no fuel for more, we wore only one outfit of clothes because we wore all our clothes at once, and many of us had to fetch every drop of water from fifty yards away. I do not recall that it made life less difficult.

Chesterton jeered at Mr Mandragon the millionaire because of the simple life he led – with the aid of a dandy little machine, with a hundred pulleys and cranks between to hoist him out of his healthful bed on every day of his life, to wash him and brush him and shave him and dress him to live the simple life. To my mind, Mr Mandragon was absolutely right; to lead the simple life one needs such a machine; and the name of the machine is civilization.

4 · *Spark and Stove*

Professor Sale of Cornell once quoted some high-flown remark of D. H. Lawrence's about life being a series of passionately felt moments; and then said: 'But life isn't like that
– you gotta get your pants pressed; got to get the diapers in
before it rains.'

The fact that getting the pants pressed on time may actually
matter in a marriage, or even that the passionate moments
may lead to diapers, is something which seems to have escaped
many of our best-educated guys and dolls. We often seem to
be in a generation which not only minds more about feeling
the right things than about doing them, but even believes
that doing *anything* deliberate about human relations may
impair the feelings. Skill is at a discount: spontaneity at a
premium.

It is easy to see how, in the Freudian era, this has come
about. The discovery of the beasts in the id cast a nasty light
on many of the more high-sounding attitudes of a hundred
years ago. Men who righteously beat small boys are suspected
of enjoying it; people who took gruel to the sick may have
been more pleased by their own piety than they were pained
by the misery they found.

Hypocrisy being rated as the eighth deadly sin, it has
displaced, cuckoo-like, the other seven; dishonesty and in-
sincerity about one's vices are made to seem worse than the
vices themselves.

Rightly distrusting hypocrisy, and knowing the harm some
inhibitions can do, people concentrate on spontaneity; and
they are particularly anxious not to take the bloom off their

emotions by thinking too much about them. It is not just that they do not apply their brains to their emotional problems – people never have – but that they feel it would be almost immoral to do so. Intelligent girls, especially, feel they owe it to themselves to make an utter muck of their private lives; and as for men . . . well, W. H. Auden wrote before the war:

> To the man in the street who, I'm sorry to say,
> Is a keen observer of life
> The word 'intellectual' suggests straight away
> A man who's untrue to his wife.

And times have not changed much since then.

The odd thing is that this Freudian-based horror of inhibition bears an extraordinary likeness to a Shelley-esque romanticism. Talk about uninhibited freedom and you find you are using the same phrases that once suggested that emotion is but a fading coal; that to preserve it leaves one with a handful of ashes. The romantics' big mistake, of course, was not realizing that the way to stop a coal fading is to clap a Cosy Stove around it and then to get going with the bellows and the paper shavings. And it is at any rate arguable that the disadvantages of All For Sex are as obvious as those of All For Love.

It is not the ideal which is wrong: we have possibly got some of the highest ideals about human relations yet devised. What is shaky is our efficiency in putting them into practice. And particularly, of course, this applies to marriage. The gentle art of not saying it till you have calmed down; the realization that though drink, danger and despair are all powerful aphrodisiacs, a stable relationship may pack a stronger long-term punch; the knowledge that people are apt to have the defects of their qualities (Whitehorn's Third Law states that no nice men are good at getting taxis); the recognition

20

that moments of either elation or disillusion can be, as Belloc said of religious doubt, 'a mood, not a conclusion': all these notions, which have nothing to do with spontaneity, have a great deal to do with staying happy though married. It never ceases to astound me that people who realize perfectly well that good cooking or good business need a great deal of care and attention, still think that a marriage should work without even the minimum upkeep of kindness, fidelity and conversation.

The hero-figures of the Freudian era are, perhaps inevitably, artists: from the Gauguin runaway in the school text of *The Moon and Sixpence* to more advanced excavators of the sub-conscious such as Lawrence and Joyce. And this is part of the trouble. We can forgive a Matisse or a Picasso for chang-ing women the way the others change shirts, because of their paintings: but their behaviour is totally inappropriate to the minor art collector who assumes the same privilege. The need for self-expression may set a Dylan Thomas above the re-strictions of common politeness, but this has absolutely nothing to do with whether a copywriter should or should not be blindingly rude to his mother-in-law. Yet his justifica-tion is, he believes, the same.

All this is confined to what one may loosely call the intelligent classes – or intelligently call the looser classes. Down at the *Woman's Own* level they are busy dishing out advice which, however woolly, is at least intended to take things as they are and make them work.

And it is among the intelligentsia (sounds like a pot-plant, that word) that this adoption of the creative ethos can have a melancholy effect on work, too. Art, irrespective of whether it is any good or not, is valued at the expense of craft: girls who could make excellent journalists feel that it is nobler to write bad novels; artistic young men, instead of building careers in which a modicum of taste might help, complain about the 'rat race' and solace themselves with painting bad abstracts in the evenings; spoiled idealists sit in bars and denounce the system and the hypocrisy of politicians, instead of getting into politics and sorting the system out.

The irony of it all is that probably real work, properly done, brings ordinary people nearer to the artistic experience than anything else – but to do it properly, one has to learn its disciplines and accept its limitations; one has to regard the whole of a human life as an artefact, a product of brains and skill and perseverance. Sure, the spark that starts it should be spontaneous – but to run one's life on that is like trying to keep warm all winter lighting matches.

5 · *Someone, Somewhere, Waiting*

Ogden Nash once complained that the sins of omission were far less jovial than the sins of commission: that nobody ever says 'The next round of unwritten letters is on me.' He had laid his finger on a point which has escaped all the authors of letter-writing manuals: that the main trouble about letters is simply getting started at all.

People are extraordinarily idiosyncratic in their ways of goading themselves to take pen in hand. A reader wrote to say that she adjourns to the Victoria Station waiting-room when the pile threatens to overflow on to the floor; presumably she wrote that letter from Victoria, too. A good many others seem to write only from hospitals – mental hospitals, one is sometimes tempted to think.

A friend of mine used to be able to get down to it only on Sundays; then he found more cheerful things to do with his Sundays and wrote only on Bank Holidays. Now things have deteriorated still further and he is having the date printed with his address on his writing-paper: it says simply, 'Christmas Day'.

My grandfather thought the Christmas Day gambit worked, too – but he let the thing run away with him to the point at which he had to begin writing his innumerable Christmas letters rather before the end of his summer holiday. My husband writes only about two proper letters a year, and those to whoever he happens to be addressing when the fit strikes him: having failed to write to his relations for months on end, he suddenly astounds his plumber with a three-page letter on the state of the nation.

My father finds no difficulty (unlike the rest of us) in getting down to writing: he just refuses to write *long* letters. A friend who once wrote him twenty closely reasoned pages on the meaning of the universe still carries around his answer: it is a postcard containing the single word 'Quite'.

Myself, I have only once got clear, and that was after spending three days and three nights on a train. What's more, I don't think I have this trains thing to myself: if Tolstoy had been the realist he's cracked up to be, I cannot help feeling, Anna Karenina wouldn't have spent all those days in the train brooding: she'd have been clearing up her correspondence like the rest of us.

Even for ardent practising letter-writers, of course, there can be letters that are hell to write. There is the letter of congratulation to the girl who has just married a man you have been steadily advising her to abandon ('I am sure you will be much happier now that you have come to a decision'); the letter trying to find out from the giver whether the set of five cups she has sent as a wedding present is one too many or one too few; the thank-you letter for a present which you absolutely cannot identify – it is always too dangerous to guess, or you find you have praised a Teasmade for its beauty or a book token as an original idea.

A friend of mine, in America on a visa which prohibited work, once had to write a very careful letter indeed to the visa authorities after she had written to them, and written to an employment agency, and put the letters in the wrong envelopes. The trickiest one I remember writing (in entirely innocent circumstances, let me say) had to read: 'Dear X, I am so happy to hear of your engagement . . . I wonder if by any chance you have found my ear-ring?'

But even when the situation is not difficult, the mere fact of not having written makes it so. Only the openings are easier, since you must always start with an apology (some

French Abbé had an even better way out: he used to start 'I cannot adequately describe the pleasure it affords me to write to you every year'). But you can never persuade your hostess that a bread-and-butter letter that is six weeks late shows how fragrantly the week-end has hung in your memory; people will never believe that you put off writing until you had time to write a *real* letter, however true it is.

Worse: if you plan to write a really savage letter and finally decide that Silence is Nobler (not to say safer) the other person will never appreciate your restraint, but will just think you never got around to writing, again.

I don't know what can be done about it all. We might try something sociable, like Five-Letters-a-Morning coffee parties – though even then I suppose one would fail to write and say if one was coming or not. It might help to have no sizes of writing-paper between the mammoth – strictly for chattering to one's family – and the tiny, which would make all letters shorter and therefore better. One might try to write three letters every day after breakfast – but then one would have to have breakfast, not to mention stamps.

What is really wanted is a sort of general amnesty, such as might be brought on by a three-month postal strike, so that it would be clear that any letters not written before were not going to be written after: we could then all clear our consciences and start clean.

But since this is impossible, I have devised a way of getting rid of thirty long personal letters in an hour. I am going to type out thirty very short notes to (say) the Gas Board, and write my friends' names on the envelopes – in my own handwriting, so that they know who it has come from. They will then assume that I have simply put two letters in the wrong envelopes, and that a long and friendly letter is for ever lost in the wilderness of the Gas Board. It will then, thank heaven, be once again their turn to write.

6 · Too Timid for Words

Many of my best friends are Roman Catholics – at least they were yesterday. I hope they still are today; for this article is not really about Roman Catholics and what they do; it is about the Protestants who fail to resist Catholic pressures.

The expert on Roman Catholic pressure, of course, is the Family Planning Association. Its history is studded with monotonously similar stories: R.C.s on local councils opposing the renting of premises for clinics; R.C.s writing to their M.P.s to protest against having family planning clinics at all; R.C.s heckling the F.P.A.'s meetings in many places where a clinic was proposed: all this has sometimes held up the opening of a clinic for years. F.P.A. publicity, too, has always been liable to take a knocking: three years ago Roman Catholic pressure succeeded in getting the most innocuous F.P.A. posters taken out of the Tubes.

In women's magazines, too, there is an oblique form of censorship. When I worked on them some years ago I was always coming up against it: I remember wanting to mention that one couple had a poodle that screamed when left alone: they had to hire someone to hold its paw; and then realized that if they were paying for a poodle-sitter anyway, they might as well go ahead and incur a baby-sitter. This whole anecdote was cut out because it implied that not having a baby had until then been voluntary. I remember, too, having a sentence removed which explained why a film star had divorced his first wife: to suggest that a divorce had a cause was tantamount, apparently, to condoning it.

What my editors were afraid of was partly the number

of people who would write in signing themselves Disgusted R.C., and partly the fear of being banned in Ireland (or of being refused by Irish distributors). This fear worries newspapers, too: emotional columnists – I mean writers of columns about the emotions – complain that they have an appalling struggle to get anything realistic about birth control or divorce into the paper. Some of the bigger papers and magazines change a few things for the Irish editions (this article, for example, did not appear in the Irish edition of *The Observer*), but most magazines have no special edition and find it easier simply to render all articles non-irritant to R.C. sensibilities.

The magazines have become a lot less nervy of late, I believe; one can only guess how much of this is due to a new fearlessness in their editors and how much to the fact that the Irish censor himself has changed his policy for the broader.

One may well wonder why a censor in Ireland should have *any* effect on what British Protestants read, and yet still not feel that the matter is particularly important; with the F.P.A. having nearly 400 clinics and every magazine finding some roundabout way of handing out a family planning pamphlet, things may not look too bad. But it matters more than might appear. For one thing 400 F.P.A. clinics is nowhere near enough – that is about the number of the Citizens' Advice Bureaux, which everyone agrees would have to be doubled to provide a reasonable coverage for consumer complaints. For another, although as the Malthusiad says

> '*The middle classes – me and you –
> Already know a thing or two*'

it is those who are most ignorant and hardest up who need the services of the F.P.A. most – and who are least likely to thread their way through the magazine euphemisms and actually write up for a pamphlet. There is plenty of evidence, too, that thousands of couples practise birth control by highly dubious methods simply because they do not know any of the better ways.

The Roman Catholic view about birth control is not, of course, by any means a static thing. There are differences in opinion between Irish Catholics and Americans, Spaniards and Britons; and the recent controversial book by Harvard's top gynaecologist, Catholic Dr John Rock, is enough to show that the interpretation of this particular doctrine is anything but finally settled. A great deal of discussion goes on among Catholics about the relative permissibility of the safe period, the Pill, *coitus reservatus* and so on. But it sometimes seems as if Catholics can debate the subject with less fear of censorship or disapproval than Protestants and Humanists.

It is not for people who are outside the Catholic Church to get mixed up in their argument, or in any way condemn them for doing what their Church enjoins. One cannot fairly complain even when they try to keep the rest of us off contraception: though even on this Catholic opinions vary, some (among them Father Laurence Bright, O.P.) thinking that this is a matter in which Catholics should leave non-Catholics alone. But the very fact that the Catholic view may turn out to be not what one had always thought makes it even more nonsensical for the rest of us to be so pussy-footed about expressing our own views; we should be establishing our own point of view irrespective of what the Roman Catholics think either way.

Part of the trouble, I am sure, is that when most of us see a Church – any Church – being militant, we tend to assume that it is simply being more righteous than the rest of us – more extreme, that is, but in the same direction. In the case of divorce there may be something in it: if you say 'Only a saint could put up with that woman' you could well say 'If I were a saint I would put up with her'.

But on birth control, the Roman Catholic view is *not* just an extreme version of the Protestant one. For Churches who think that physical love is divinely intended to express spiritual love and that it is wrong to produce more children than one can look after properly, family planning is not only not a sin, it is, in the words of one bishop, 'a right and important factor in Christian family life'. And for the even vaster numbers of ordinary humane agnostics the position is simpler still: if Roman Catholic opposition to birth control is responsible for even a tenth of our botched back-street abortions, unhappy forced marriages and illegitimate children, then their influence is something which should be fought as a downright evil.

Heaven knows we do not want to go back to religious persecution; the days are happily over when a hysterical newspaper accused Cosmo Lang of 'practising celibacy in the open street'. But I think it might even things up a bit if we had an anti-Catholic lobby exactly equal in strength to the Catholic one; they would then simply cancel out, and editors and administrators would have nothing to lose by going by their own good sense and consciences, or, in default of either, at least by the majority of their readers and voters and not just the most vocal minority.

We have licensing laws; we have Sunday-observance laws; we have the Archbishop of Canterbury sitting in the Lords. For better or (possibly) worse, we are officially a Protestant country. Nobody ought to deny Roman Catholics the right to live according to their religion; but it is time we stopped being so chary of offending their sensibilities that we let the opposition case go by default. Only when Protestant countries are prepared to make as much fuss *for* birth control as the Catholic countries do against it will there be any hope of limiting the numbers of those who are born only to starve to death; and militancy begins at home.

7 · *Missing Marriage Lines*

'They spend five guineas on a hat, drive thirty miles, drink two glasses of champagne and go away again,' said the bride's mother wonderingly. 'It's extraordinary when you come to think of it.'

The whole business of weddings is extraordinary; and I find as time goes on one comes to think of it in a series of monotonously repeated questions. Why does not the bride's family simply hire 100 hats and lob them out at random as the guests enter the church, since it always looks as if this is what has happened, anyway?

Why does not the Church of England maintain a special flying squad of parsons specializing in weddings, parsons trained not to address a mixed wedding audience as if it were a mission school or a football match, nor to ruin the atmosphere with ill-timed cracks about confetti in the churchyard?

Why do the poor fathers seem to take it harder than anybody, and go round perspiring, introducing men to their own wives and lighting cigarettes at the filter end? Why is it that those who are happily married always weep the hardest?

And why do people buy the hats, and send the presents, and drive the distance out of genuine good will, only to spend the time making catty remarks about the arrangements, the other guests or (as in my case) the hats and the parsons?

Whatever the lunacies of the *bombe glacée* wedding, though, there is more to be said for it than one might think. To start with it acts, just because it *is* a long and elaborate process, as a species of brake, making it just that much harder to get married in a rush of temporary enthusiasm or a fit of absence of mind.

Again, the mere fact of gathering a familiar mob around one to witness the deed has its uses: whereas (I have always felt) one could marry almost anybody in the privacy of a registry office, the knowledge that one has to fling the spouse down like a glove, so to speak, saying 'This is what I want – this is what I am like – this is where I stand' to a couple of hundred people is apt to give one furiously to think.

And since, however close the previous arrangements may have been, being married is not in the least like not being married, there is something to be said for having some sort of fuss or ceremonial to emphasize the fact. A child wakes up *feeling* nine on his ninth birthday, but a grown-up can really feel much the same two days after being married as two days before – unless the time before all the fuss started can artificially be made to seem several light-years away.

What always intrigues me as I watch them gulping out 'I do' is the thought of all the other contracts they are making without realizing it. The parson could hardly say 'Dost thou, Algernon, promise to laugh at this woman's jokes, push the car until it starts and bring her sherry in her bath?' and the congregation would be surprised to hear the bride whispering 'I do' to the proposition that she should keep quiet at breakfast, find the things her husband has put down only a minute ago, dash it, and refrain from telling his employer what she thinks of him. Yet these are the agreements which really give a marriage its shape.

One difficulty about so reconstructing the marriage service would be, of course, that one rarely knows ahead what this sort of agreement is going to be. There was no way for a relation of mine to know beforehand that her husband got married mainly to have someone there to do something when the laundry sent back his pyjamas with the cord lost half-way round the back; nor for the friend who married a dashing naval officer to know that she would spend the rest of her life nursing his TB in a remote country village, still less that she would enjoy it.

A Catholic chum knew of his bride's willingness to bear him absolutely any number of children, but could hardly have realized that a condition of this was that she should not be asked to cook while pregnant. No one could have told my husband and me (well, at any rate, no one *did*) that our most important type of crisis behaviour would be keeping afloat during our numerous alternating (and even, on occasion, coinciding) periods of unemployment.

There may be pitfalls in finding out, too late, what the bargain really is; but a good deal more probably result from one or other party simply assuming that the contract is the same for everyone, that 'every' man does this, 'every' woman must do that. Tolstoy's view that all happy families are happy in the same way may have something in it when it comes to children, the great levellers; but as between men and women it is nonsense.

Even the most obvious generalities can be meaningless for any particular couple: for instance, few would hesitate to assert that tidiness and punctuality are useful – yet if either of us had married someone like that we'd have been crazed inside a year.

I know two marriages, both happy, which have so far departed from the norm that in one the man insists that his wife make all the decisions, including buying houses (I admit he is a poet) and in the other the man actually answers the invitations – yet neither has sustained psychological damage. Half the screams from both sides that accompany any chat about our national morals are the result of everybody thinking their own sexual formula is the only one that works. It ain't necessarily so.

Possibly the honouring of contracts is one of the few moral principles that anyone, with or without religious conviction or political convictions, would accept; and this being the case it might be interesting to look more closely at the contracts. My father refused to let me say 'obey' because he didn't believe in people promising things they had no intention of performing (not that I don't, dammit); and possibly far too many men promise to forsake all other without admitting that that includes blondes, while too many women agree to the cherishing without thinking the thing through in terms of darning, cocoa and hot fomentations.

It would be interesting to establish an extra contract, a pretty piece of vellum on which the couple could fill out their own contract for themselves; it could, by mutual consent, be added to, amended or revised; but its very existence would prove that while the keeping of contracts is a powerful glue, no two people stick together in quite the same way.

8 · Just You Wait, 'Enery 'Iggins

Tread softly, because you tread on my dreams – and a pretty squdgy mass you have underfoot at that. Emerging starry-eyed and embarrassed from a review of all the tales I have been talking myself to sleep with since I was a child, I hardly know whether to be more horrified at the saccharine quality of most of it or at the raw Sicilian vindictiveness of the rest. I only hope, therefore, that everyone will accept my proposition: that a woman's dream life, as much as Walter Mitty's, is always about the exact opposite of what she is up to in reality.

What she dreams about is what she cannot get. What I couldn't get at the very earliest age was a houseboat. I would spend bedtime after bedtime planning it out in every detail – the lights and the lockers and the tablecloths and the picnic baskets; I even designed tasteful green and white bathing dresses to be worn upon it by those of my family who were sufficiently in my favour at the time to be allowed on board. I need hardly say that I had never actually *seen* a houseboat, and suffered, then as now, from instant seasickness; but the idea of a floating home was strong within me. Occasionally it was supplanted by a parallel plan of owning a caravan, but religion dealt that one a blow from which it hardly recovered. One day in Sunday school we were asked to draw the caravan in which one or other of the children of Israel (or possibly Judah) had crossed the desert. I remember experiencing that tingling feeling you get at any age when the conversation comes round to your subject; and I set to work to draw my dream caravan, only making the windows narrower at the

British Consul, covers his retreat to the yacht, and races after him. She scrambles on board; he speaks to her from the darkness, moved by her display of loyalty . . . as the ancient steers the boat for the open sea, she walks down the darkened ladder into his arms. Versions of that vary quite a bit, too.

The idyll follows; and idylls make poor stuff for dreams. So we flash fairly quickly to the time when he is insisting that he cannot distort the life-pattern of one so young, and she returns to her parents, a stuffy, upper-class lot utterly unlike, I may say, my own set. For four years she trudges through the sub-deb life of her kind; comes her twenty-first dance and she elects to have it in an uncle's house on the cliffs of Cornwall; as a mark of eccentric despair, she insists on wearing black velvet for the occasion. All is dust and ashes to her, and in the middle of the ziz-boom she slinks off to a little music room overlooking the sea, and listlessly taps out 'We'll go no more a-roving' with one finger on the grand piano. Suddenly the glass door to the sea slams open; the wind blows in and there, framed by the darkness, is the pirate, looking more like Laurence Olivier than ever. He carries her off, this time finally and legally; and once aboard the lugger she is fine.

This was not, of course, the only lump of marshmallow; there was one about a woman leaving her husband and coming back, no vows broken; and another about a girl and a tall, shy coloured man, and another about a Ruritanian Princess who falls in love with a huntsman – though this one, to my disgust, went hard-centred on me and ended, after the Revolution, with them facing each other greyly across the devastated earth with absolutely nothing to say to each other. But the focus of them all was the same: the moment of discovery. From Jane Austen to *Woman*, it is the moment of reversal, when ill fortunes change to good, that is the essential of escape fiction; and a good half of the plot mechanics of this sort of thing consist simply in setting up a situation, that shall not be too obviously preposterous, in which both parties can manage to be fully committed to each other without either realizing the state the other is in (this is why inequalities of race or social standing are useful). In real life, of course, this absolutely never happens, girls always knowing ages before a man proposes so much as a dinner date, let alone the altar; but it is easy to see why it is so vital to dream life. You spin these fantasies when you are yourself less loved than you would like; to make the heroine ignorant of the burning passion which is about to flare up and ignite her is to tell one's subconscious that there may be a Romeo, even now, lurking in the shrubbery of one's own life.

I puzzled a bit over the piracy element, but I think that too is explicable in terms of wanting what you cannot have. Girls read adventurous books just as boys do, they too absorb *Autobiography of a Super-Tramp* or *Travels with a Donkey*; but they themselves are unfitted for the picturesquely picaresque: for the one feminine disadvantage which no amount of female suffrage can remove is that women can get raped. So it is travels with a revolver in the Cevennes, if at all; drifting, for those of us who insist on doing it, has to be done in slow motion, with jobs here and jobs there and no nonsense about riding the rails in between; and even hitch-hiking, which we all do and brag about it afterwards, is no fun at the time. French driving is frightening anyway; one is always scared of French lasciviousness; and the double worry about what the lechery will do to the driving makes travel in such circumstances a horror. The only conceivable vagrant life is one you can share with a tough protector; and since the men you actually meet always want to do *their* tramping either alone or in a ruggedly masculine atmosphere, the shared adventure remains a daydream. Ask any wife of any adventurer.

It has to be admitted that marriage is a great barrier to exciting daydreams, even for those who do not talk in their sleep. There is little point in dreaming about a man who is lying only a foot away, and if he happens to be what you want, there is equally little point in dreaming about anyone else. Even the artificially constructed dreams of 'What would I do if I had a million pounds?' or 'What would I do if I had only a year to live?' lose whatever vitality they ever had when the chances are that one does not want to do anything very different from what one is doing already. So one is pretty well reduced to dreaming about work, writing imaginary letters, and slicing up one's enemies.

My favourite work dream consists of constructing the ideal magazine, on which all my old friends from the *Spectator* would work, but with shining improvements: Brian Inglis would write about bugs as well as bogies, Monica Furlong would go back to reporting with affectionate amusement on the antics of the Church of England, Bernard Levin would relight his Taper, and I, personally, would have the joy of cutting down all articles on foreign subjects from three columns to one and a half. Sometimes this ideal magazine links up with my other secret indulgence, and becomes the instrument through which I expose the hypocrisy and evil intentions of my enemies; but mostly my revenge on them has a more personal flavour: I am refusing a dime for a cup of coffee to a man who once sacked me, or being in a position to see that someone who once sued me for libel never gets a respectable job again. Sometimes the ideal revenge I plan simply consists in pairing them off, and I revel in visions of Lady Hulton unexpectedly married to Sir Henry Brooke.

When, as so often happens, one's enemy is also one's employer, one spends a lot of time composing a letter of resignation designed to bring home to him not only the rottenness of his organization but also the extent of the talent he is now losing; and when, as is the case at the moment, one actually likes one's employers, a substitute has to be found. My favourite has been the letter I imagined resigning from the circle of Fashion Editors, explaining exactly why I never want to look at another dress show in any circumstances ever again so long as I live.

These letters, I suppose, are the direct descendants of the ones one used to write in one's head when single, the interminable letter to explain, accuse, demolish, forgive or assimilate the hurts and strains of the *affaire de cœur* just ending. These one sometimes did actually write and post, though the consequences were always disastrous; either they had to be returned unread because the chap had by then married someone else, or they had the effect of starting the whole thing up again, and upon my Sam I don't know which was worse. It is odd, now I come to think about it, that the enemies arranged for a carve-up of the imagination never seem to include old boy friends. Either it is all too long ago and far away, I suppose, or one is, in retrospect, so appalled at what would have happened if they *hadn't* behaved like snakes that one forgives them.

Letters can often take the place of straight wish-fulfilment: you dare not dream of being engaged, but you phrase and re-phrase the letter breaking the glad news to your mother ('Tell her,' said my husband unfeelingly when it actually happened, 'that I'm unemployed, penniless, and have the chest of a boy of fourteen and the lungs of a man of ninety'). For dreaming directly about what you actually hope may happen is something, I think, that few women have the courage to do. They are far too superstitious: too accurate a visualization would work as a bad magic and make sure you never got the thing in the end. It is far too dangerous to think about the college entrance, the first job, the wedding ring, the filled cradle – one can only look at them out of the corner of one's eye, working out the clothes one would need, or where one should live, or how the finances of it might work out.

Which is simply another proof that the secret life and the real one must never meet. The secret life is a strange garden on the far side of the mirror, peopled by gods and demons; and hopes that are planted there will catch unreality like a sickness and fade and die. It works the other way round too, of course: sometimes one does not want one's secret life upset by reality. I nearly met one of my enemies at a party the other day and had to leave abruptly: I might actually have said something civil to the man, and *then* what about that dream of spitting in his eye?

9 · *Words, Words, Words*

'In this *materialistic* age, when the forces of *so-called* moderni-
zation ensure that the teenager is bombarded with sex, it is
hardly surprising that the standards of a *more leisured age* are
vanishing.'

This sentence, which appears in the letters column of most
popular dailies about three times a week, contains a fair
sample of words used as a smoke-screen. 'Leisured age', for a
start, is the euphemism for a society in which housemaids and
factory hands worked fourteen hours a day – and euphemism
is probably the commonest verbal contortion. In industry,
they tell me, 'unfair competition' is competition you cannot
meet, and 'free enterprise' a condition where the Government
regulations ensure that you make money; while the Japanese
go in widely for a form of price-fixing known as 'orderly
marketing'.

In the dress trade, 'a useful little dress' means one with no
distinguishing characteristics; 'romantic' means 'cleft to the
waist'. 'Company director' or 'model' are useful euphemisms
for those who appear in dubious court cases, and nobody
minds except the model agencies; nor can it be long now, I
feel, before someone sues a columnist for describing her as
someone's 'great and good friend' – the beauty of such a case
being, of course, that she would have to prove that 'mistress'
was what the phrase *had* meant in its previous 4,583 appear-
ances in the column.

One of the snags of euphemism, of course, is that it can
destroy the phrase for use in its original sense. The Victorian
lover who said, 'Miss Shuttlecock, you must be aware that I

have long entertained for you feelings warmer than those of ordinary friendship' left no phrase for a real and delicious condition which is exactly *not* what you feel when you love someone to the point of marriage. The hypocritical 'many of my best friends are Jews', now almost synonymous with anti-semitism, leaves no way of describing someone (e.g. me) of whose ten closest friends six actually are Jewish.

There is an Orwellian grimness about the naming of the Abolition of Passes Act in South Africa, which ensured that an African had to carry twenty-seven papers combined into one booklet; or the Extension of University Education Act, whose effect was to keep black Africans out of the two hitherto desegregated universities. Female circumcision, the anthropologist's phrase for a widespread barbaric practice, though strictly accurate, serves to conceal a mutilation that would be better understood if it was called female castration; and the cheery Z-cars phrase 'a bit of G.B.H.' (grievous bodily harm) at least lets you off imagining the split cheeks and teeth all over the road.

Our own post-war speciality, I think, is the pessimism. The opposite of euphemism, it is a Pavlovian signal for the secre-tion of adrenalin. My pet hate among these is 'rat-race'. People condemn the rat-race for forcing them to catch the 8.15, stand one another business lunches and worry about promotion – which rats, actually, almost never do. Sometimes the phrase condemns a man's perfectly legitimate attempt to rise in his profession. More often it is used to blame the system for the fact that a man is simply working for the money: there is nothing actually to *stop* him going back to subsistence fishing, after all; he would just rather not.

Again, 'keeping up with the Joneses' usually tells you noth-ing except that the old middle class are furious to see the new adopting decent standards of homemaking (you have only to read Thackeray's *Book of Snobs* to realize how passionately the

Victorians competed with their neighbours). This emotion, indeed, produces a whole crop of such misapplied words: 'materialistic' means 'richer', especially as applied to Americans: the British housewife spends her time cooking and cleaning for her family, making the house look attractive and worrying about education; the American housewife does exactly the same things but with better equipment: ergo, she is materialistic.

'Teenage', too, has long since ceased to mean girls and boys from thirteen to nineteen: it has become a horror word for the jeans, the Beatles, the revolt, the Enemy. 'Everybody' or 'nobody' simply indicates 'us', as in 'nobody has servants any more' (really?). 'They' is a good word for side-stepping personal responsibility, and with it can be coupled 'we' in such sentences as 'We ought to force these blighters to surrender'. The only sensible come-back to this is to ask 'Who, exactly? You – or someone else?'.

Then there is the category of words whose meaning has been spread so thinly it hardly has substance any more. For example, as soon as you suggest that *everything* you approve of has a particular quality – as with Leavis's use of 'moral', or 'progressive' in the old *New Statesman* – the word has no other meaning except 'good'. Such words as 'freedom' and 'reality' still have enough body in them to be worth arguing about – though 'realistic' can vary from its theatre meaning of 'with damp washing' to its place at the top of the conjugation 'I am realistic, you have compromised, he has sold out'.

'Democracy' is now just about useless except as an emotive noise. As for 'natural', it means exactly what anyone wants it to mean. It can mean 'clothes that were in fashion ten years ago' – though rarely the hides of the first savage or the carved nose-ornament of the second; it can mean a set of highly tricky breathing exercises as in 'natural childbirth'. I have often wanted to start a discussion about the meaning of 'natural' between a Roman Catholic who believed in natural methods of family planning and in curing the world's food shortage by technology, and a nature-food devotee who wants nothing but natural fertilizers used to speed up agriculture.

Maybe we would have more fun, and kick a little more vigour into the language, if instead of distorting old words we simply evolved new ones. I could no more get along now without my word 'practics' – meaning getting down to it and sorting out all the boring practical details ('Right, we go to Italy in May. The rest is a question of practics') – than Barbara Griggs could do without *her* self-explanatory word 'insinuendo'. And even if one cannot quite approve of 'psychoceramics' (the study of cracked pots) there is everything to be said for that splendid engineer's word for an imprecise calculation that tells you whether it is worth going ahead to a precise one: 'guestimate'.

If you make your own words up, other people may not know what on earth you mean; but at least *you* do; and that is half the battle. The real trouble about woolly and wrongly used words is not that (as Voltaire said of speech generally) they conceal our thoughts. It is that they effectively stop us thinking properly at all.

10 · *Sluts – I*

This article is dedicated to all those who have ever changed their stockings in a taxi, brushed their hair with someone else's nailbrush or safety-pinned a hem; and those who have not had probably better not read on.

Anyone in doubt, however, can ask herself the following questions. Have you ever taken anything back out of the dirty-clothes basket because it had become, relatively, the cleaner thing? How many things are there, at this moment, in the wrong room – cups in the study, boots in the kitchen; and how many of them are on the *floor* of the wrong room?

Could you try on clothes in any shop, any time, without worrying about your underclothes? And how, if at all, do you clean your nails? Honest answers should tell you, once and for all, whether you are one of us: the miserable, optimistic, misunderstood race of sluts.

We are not ordinary human beings who have degenerated, as people think: we are born this way. Even at four you can pick us out: the little girls in the playground who have one pant-leg hanging down and no hair-slide; at ten we are the ones who look dirty even when we are clean (unlike the goodigoodies who look unfairly clean when they are dirty); and at fifteen, when black stockings are fashionable, we betray ourselves in the changing-room by legs spotted like a Dalmatian's, the inevitable result of using Indian ink instead of darning-wool.

People who are not sluts intolerantly assume that we must like things this way, without realizing the enormous effort and inconvenience that goes into being so ineffective: the number of times we have to fill the car's radiator because we don't get it mended, the fortunes we spend on taxis going back for parcels we have left in shops, the amount of ironing occasioned by our practice of unpacking not so much when we get back from a week-end as four days later.

We acquire, it is true, certain off-beat skills: I am much better at holding a bottle of varnish between two fingers than those of my friends who do not paint their nails in the Tube, and they cannot cut their nails with a pen-knife, either; but nothing really makes up to us for the difficulties of our way of life.

However, I am not trying to make a soggy bid for sympathy so much as to work out what we can possibly do to improve our condition. And the first thing, it seems to me, is to inscribe *Abandon Hope All Ye Who Enter Here* over the lintels of all our messy houses; for it is our optimism that is principally our undoing. We keep hoping that we will remember to wash our white collars, or find time to comb our hair on the way to the office, or slide into the building and dump our coats before anyone can see that there are three buttons missing. More, it seems to me, could be done if we could only face up realistically to all the things we never will be able to do.

We can realize, for example, that no power on earth is going to make us look well turned out all, or even most, of the time. We can therefore give up right away any New Year resolutions about fashion: a second pair of little white gloves will simply result in our carrying two right hands; wigs would be a waste of money because those of us who cannot keep our real hair tidy cannot keep our toy hair tidy either. Instead, we can wear reasonably sober clothes normally, go for stacked heels because we know we won't remember to get them re-heeled before they are worn down, have only one colour of accessories, so that we cannot wear the brown shoes with the black bag.

And, having accepted that people are *not* going to say 'she's always so chic', we can concentrate every now and then on really dazzling efforts that will knock our audience sideways. Jane Austen was right when she said that no beauty accustomed to compliments ever got anything like the thrill of an ordinary looker who was told she was looking terrific *that evening*.

We can give up making good resolutions about replacing things before they run out, which is absurd, and concentrate instead on bulk buying, so that the gap between supply and supply happens much more rarely. We can also, of course, keep icing sugar, the wrong sort of rice, tea bags, spearmint toothpaste and so on specifically to tide us over when we do run out of the real thing. It is true that we tend not to have any money either, but as we usually spend what we have at the beginning of the month like drunken sailors anyway, we might as well spend it on vast tubs of cleansing cream, acres of Kleenex (which we have to have, since clean handkerchiefs, let's face it, are beyond us), sugar in ten-pound bags.

Apart from this sort of grim realism, there are, I think, only two other things that can help us. The first is habit: odd as it may seem, even sluts do occasionally acquire good habits (we clean our teeth, for example, even if we sometimes have to do it with soap) and these, indeed, are all that hold us together. A slut who baths whenever she has time never baths at all: her only hope is to get up into one every morning; if she shops here and there for food there will never be any around, but a Saturday supermarket raid will settle a whole week's hash at one go.

And the second is money: for the only way a slut can really get things done is to get someone else to do them. Even the most domestic slut will find it worth earning a few pounds to pay for help in the house.

The only way to make up for missing the post is a long-distance telephone call; the only way not to have to go back to fetch things is to get them picked up by messenger. The only thing that will get a slut's carpets vacuumed daily is a daily. All sluts ought to be, or to marry, rich people: and I treasure the hope that among the really rich there may be dozens of sluts lurking undetected by the rest.

Money, low cunning and a sense of realism may help us somewhat; but it is a hard life all the same. I wrote this article two years ago, but as it was felt that it hardly came well from the pen of a fashion editor, it was never printed. So I thought I had a soft option using it now; except that, of course, I couldn't find it, and have had to write the whole blasted thing again.

11 · Sluts – II

A couple of months ago I owned up in this column to being a slut. It was absolutely splendid: I found that there were scores of us, all struggling away.

There was the woman who had got to be a dab hand at identifying lettuce in the dark, as she never remembered to pick it by daylight; and the one who said she couldn't have a daily help – it was too much effort clearing up before she came. There was one who cited her six children as proof of her sluthood, in one direction at least; and the mother who claimed that (thanks to a scarf in the wrong washing-machine load) her baby was the only one in Ruislip with blue nappies.

Men, too – they call it 'slob': one wrote in block capitals by candlelight having run out of shillings for the meter, and another said he stapled his braces to his trousers when all buttons failed.

Some sluts had come to terms with their state: 'We now live on a small yacht; it solves a lot of problems' – presumably much of the mess simply falls over the side and is washed away. Others were still protesting: '*Why* are there no three-way mirrors even in first-class carriages?' A good many offered suggestions on thwarting the second law of thermodynamics which is the tendency of everything in the universe towards dissolution and decay.

Their suggestions were colourful to the point of being lurid. There was this business of keeping suspenders going when the bobble is off: many rejected aspirins, on the ground that sluts never have any (but use gin for headaches instead), and instead advocated corn rings and coins; one said, 'I used the buttons off my husband's pyjamas till he sewed them on again.'

Shoulder straps can be kept going with a paperclip, and one woman even suggested that if both straps have gone you can keep a slip up by wearing your bra outside it. (To my mind, one should go in for vests and slips that are strapless on purpose, I mean made that way, and stay up accordingly.)

Plainly, sluts should not wear seamed nylons, as it is the seams that usually betray the fact that the stockings are not a pair – and ladders show less in pale than in patterned stockings. Sluts should get all necessary hems shortened at the time of purchase, since they will never actually get around to doing it themselves; and, apropos of hems, they should keep a ready supply of black safety pins.

Many would agree that colourless pearl nail varnish shows chips less than coloured – but if the varnish is to hide London grime as well, three coats per nail is a minimum. For any dress that has a little white collar, a slut should also buy some white beads, for the collar's off-days; and all sluts should have bathroom curtains made of towelling for the times when the guest is in the bathroom but the towels are in the hot-cupboard.

Sluts have special problems in the kitchen. Any slut must at all costs avoid a pressure cooker, or sooner or later she will leave it too long (like all those other blackened pans) and blow herself up. She needs a lot of Kleenex, both for sitting a cup on when the saucer is sloppy, and for wiping round a pan out of which fat has spilled: if you don't, as I know from bitter experience, the fat down the side of the pan acts as a fuse to the gas and the whole thing goes up in a sheet of flame.

One slut asserts sadly that 'you cannot make white sauce with custard powder'; another recommends double sinks – so that when one is stacked with dirty crocks you can still wash the cup you need in the other. I myself am a great believer in wooden plates since you cannot break them; though I have to admit that you can – I have – set them on fire.

When it comes to entertaining, sluts should beware the *second* time. The first time you cook anything, you go carefully and may get it right; the second, the chances are you think you remember it better than you do or overcorrect on small faults; and disaster follows.

No slut could be expected to keep a hostess book, but one book which is useful is a book like an address-book as a check on all other cookery books: you look up veal, say, and it gives you your six different recipes with the books they come in and page numbers. This begins by being exactly the sort of pointless time-consuming piece of reorganization that sluts love, and ends by being an effective way of stopping you either cooking the same thing over and over, or embarking on the right dish but the wrong recipe.

Sluts should buy stamped envelopes, as half of them never have stamps and the other half never have envelopes; they should go in for string bags because their overloaded paper carriers always burst.

Those who have desks can stratify the mess on them by putting a layer of newspaper over it all and starting again – the dates on the newspapers then tell the slut what the paleolithic shells tell the geologist (though one don in Cambridge who does this is said to have buried his umbrella on his desk – open).

One could go on for ever. No one was able to suggest a way in which sluts could cure themselves of the disease known in my home town as 'doing a Whitehorn' – taking endless trouble to save yourself trouble, so that you clean an oil-lamp rather than walk to the corner of the road to buy a new bulb, or throw cushions at a door for ten minutes rather than get up and shut it.

The only serious spur to tidying up is generally agreed to

be visitors – the only drawback being that after they have gone your Pelmanism has to be even better than usual if you are ever to find anything again. But sluts are good at using memory as a substitute for tidiness – though I absolutely deny that I ever said (as friends allege): 'If you're looking for the tax forms they're under your slippers in the salad-bowl.'

12 · *Jungle on the Hearth*

Since one of my cats has eczema and the other has worms *The Observer* has temporarily lifted the ban it normally imposes on my writing about pets. Small danger this week, it feels, of a gush of sentimentality about God's Furry Creatures; and they are dead right.

There is probably hardly an animal, now I come to think about it, that is without its revolting side. Goldfish get fungus. Cats, even when fit (yes, yes, I admit it), smell. Budgerigars are more stupid than one would believe possible – put two virgin birds of opposite sex in a cage together and they *never get the message* – there was a male who lived in the flat beneath us whose wildest thrill for years was to kiss his female and then run up a little ladder and proudly ring a bell. They finally died, to the relief of all, by knocking their water-tray over on top of themselves and perishing beneath it.

Ants, of all things, have periodic patches in vogue: the problem is to feed them without letting them out of their (careful how you pronounce it) formicarium. One way is a syringe: 'Be sure you tell the chemist what you want it for,' warned one husband as his wife went out to buy one: to which she replied bitterly that she would much rather the man thought she was a drug addict.

The most obvious failing of dogs seems to be that they are so often ardent fetishists who take every chair-leg, suitcase, cushion or knee for their object. During the fuss in which Arthur Koestler tried to get the Government to relax the quarantine regulations, one man I know said he thought the Government kept the regulations going deliberately just to

53

stop people taking their dogs abroad: 'The British are quite unpopular enough already.'

Considering what absolutely rotten public relations pets do for their owners and what a nuisance and expense they are, one finds oneself increasingly wondering why people own them at all (unless they married into them, as I did). Some people keep them to have someone to talk to, I suppose; and they do have some value as a kind of half-way mark between things and people. Yell at a child, and you can kid yourself the discipline is for its moral welfare; yell at a cat, which has no moral sense and no way of getting one, and you know you are simply letting off steam. Some virtues, too, can be practised on animals: once you have lost a rabbit or two by failing to feed them at regular intervals, you are unlikely to do the same thing to the baby.

And there is, of course, the private colonialism of extending one's control over a wider empire: I know one harassed London kitten who stands in lieu of ten acres, three horses and a cow to its flat-trapped owners.

They may even, as one Trinidadian put it, 'Fill the gap left by the abolition of slavery': and satisfy the desire to own another life. And I used to think it was this desire to control and dominate that was the main reason people kept pets – pet-owners are distinguished from naturalists mainly, after all, by their insistence that the pet shall lead their lives rather than vice versa.

But you have only to look around and see how little control actually is exercised by pet-owners to make nonsense of this theory; and I have recently come to the conclusion that it is just the other way round. The real appeal of pets is simply that they cannot be altogether controlled. To keep a pet is to retain a piece of incalculable jungle in an otherwise ordered existence. The pugs at fashion shows are brought along, I am sure, in the subconscious hope that they will bite the frills of the rag trade; the old lady has a parrot because, deep down in her clean, devoted soul, she hopes it *will* speak a rude word in front of the vicar. My in-laws keep vast, intractable dogs in an otherwise respectable suburb: I am convinced they secretly wait for the day on which the animals will go wild and ravage the neighbourhood.

My favourite newsclipping concerns an old dear who was in trouble with the neighbours for keeping upwards of fifty cats: 'An inspector who called was unable to take an exact count,' it said, and you can just see the poor fellow wading hopelessly through them. Perhaps it was their unbridled fertility that appealed to her.

The other evening a man was telling me about his coming of age: downstairs there were debs, flowers, candles, but up-stairs their bitch was on heat. His mother was embarrassed by the line of thin yellow dogs panting outside the window and told someone to shoo them away. But the boy who opened the window to flap his napkin at them was borne down by a yelping tide of uncontrollable animals belting upstairs. . . . I suspect this is what pet-owners secretly hope for, and that the pets we all really want are the Gadarene swine.

13 · He that Hath Ears, Let Him Talk

It is a moot point whether people suffer worst if the disadvantages they struggle under are obvious to all, like weighing twenty-four stone or having an albatross around the neck; or if they are invisible, like gallstones or a guilty conscience. But certainly the invisible ailments are the more likely to be misunderstood by others; and one of the most misunderstood is deafness.

Bandage your eyes for a day, and the drawbacks are immediate: you cannot read or write and you bump into things. Put plugs in your ears, however, and all you may feel to begin with is a welcome absence of the noise of other people's sports cars. Yet in the long run deafness is just as bad as blindness, because it cuts one off from *people*.

A blind person does not make *us* uncomfortable. We may help him across a road, but otherwise he demands no more of the rest of us than he would if he could see. But deafness incommodes us with the effort to make ourselves understood – so most of us simply make three minutes' polite conversation and then talk to someone else. Add that up over a lifetime and it makes a pit of loneliness.

The National Health Service would be justified, to my mind, if only by the number of people who heard voices for the first time in twenty-five years with a free hearing aid; but there are plenty of forms of deafness to which even the best machine can give only, in the old phrase, all aid short of help.

Sign language is no use unless the other person knows the

signs – which means, in practice, only other deaf people or those who have spent long hours ignoring the sermon in school chapel. Even lip-reading has snags. It is hard to follow a general conversation – whatever the spy stories say, no one can read a bearded stranger across a darkened café. And much of it remains guesswork: 'The beer pail is a-fillin'' being literally indistinguishable from 'The mere male is a villain' – so it works only if the deaf person is fairly bright.

Whatever the method, talking to the deaf does take some imagination – if only to realize that they do not all need the same thing. Some, for example, hear voices better across other noises (unlikely as that seems): when my mother was going deaf there was a stage when she was at her best in the Tube, and some of the most ardent crises of our adolescence had to be discussed at the tops of our voices going round and round and round the Inner Circle. If someone has a hearing aid, there is more point in clarity than in bellowing – which simply makes you sound like those station voices announcing that the boo-fifteen will leave from platform blah.

What you say can be as important as how you speak it: it helps if you begin with the subject you are going to talk about, and if you get stuck repeat the whole phrase, and not just one word – monosyllables are hard to take in, and re-phrasing a thing in childish language only makes things worse – it's their hearing that is dicey, not their understanding.

Even people with aids need to see the speaker, and lip-readers need a good light and steady speech – which might seem too obvious to mention, except that it is always my mother's most intelligent friends who seem least capable of slowing down, facing front and taking the fag out of their mouths when they address her. And the deaf person must know a conversation is going to start, so that he can turn on the aid, put on his glasses, stop filling a hot-water bottle or whatever – I remember a conversation between one man and his deaf wife: 'We were quarrelling. . . .' 'Oh, James, we weren't *quarrelling*!' 'Well, *I* was, but you wouldn't look!'

Too often, indeed, the deaf do give the impression that they are refusing to look, rejecting contact – but this is just the defensive shell of anyone who has been snubbed too often. My mother, who is an ace lip-reader, says people are incredibly kind if you say straight out – 'I'm deaf. Please speak slowly.'

'The trouble is that it doesn't show,' one of them said. 'It would almost be easier if your ears turned purple or something.' At least purple ears would stop the commonest affront the deaf have to take: that people, misunderstanding their deafness, think they are stupid. We do the same to foreigners if we are not careful: and most of us know the gloom of being in a country where we hardly know the language – for a few minutes people speak to us like children and then the talk rockets on and leaves us out altogether. In this, the deaf are strangers in their own country for ever.

The troubles of the deaf are not, primarily, to be solved by money and good works. Of course it is nice when a hard-of-hearing group gets a minibus to tootle it around the countryside and deaf children's schools need money for equipment and teachers. But even the National Deaf Children's Society reckons that the attitude of hearing people is the core of the problem. If people included them in, deafness would be a bearable disability. As it is, it is one of the worst. So send no money, knit no blankets, get up no church bazaars. Just *talk* to them. That'll do it.

14 · A Glass of Wine in Gyney

The food, it had to be admitted, was good. That is, we all agreed that if one got it in a restaurant one would never go there again, but for a hospital it was splendid.

It was also, by definition, accompanied by yards of bread, pints of tea and a tidal wave of thick, unidentifiable soup; it arrived – or seemed to arrive – at two-hourly intervals; it was absolutely irresistible. We lay there and got fatter and fatter, and not with hospital food alone.

Almost everyone had boxes of chocolates or sweets to eat between meals, or a mound of intimidating oranges to carve up with a nail-file. One of the most cheering things about a gynaecological ward – known to the rest of the hospital as 'Gyney' – is that there is no one without visitors or snacks or flowers, which is reasonable enough, when you think what we were in for.

We were all, in fact, in for much the same thing; we were the week-end's intake of miscarriages; we all went through much the same stages at much the same time. For the first day or two, one was too woozy to talk, the blessed sleeping-pill providing oblivion; the nurses were hushed and attentive and as strict as archangels.

As one gradually sat up and took notice one got to know the people in the beds opposite first, because you could see them without turning round; the rest remained mere voices for days. The nurses developed personalities: the vague Irish nurse who looked as if she would lose the syringe and miss your arm but was in fact the best one at injections; the tall, competent Spanish nurse who had a way of saying 'Bayeebee' which started everyone weeping all over again; the great stiff-fronted hulk who was always saying: 'You didn't come here for a holiday, you know.'

On my second night there a girl was brought in who was all but dying. Fussily, like grannies, we resented her noises: the anxious hastening of nurses' creaky feet, the swinging of bed-curtains, her own appallingly genuine groans, which sounded like stage groans because really awful human feelings are like that – dramatic, unwelcome, rather absurd. She was a young painter in her twenties who had been doing a mural in a Chelsea café; she had fallen off her ladder and was having a nearly fatal miscarriage of a much-wanted illegitimate baby.

Next day, we were ashamed; we realized what a state she was in – the dripping transfusion and her putty-white face were enough to tell us. But she recovered with incredible speed; two mornings later she was making up her face at six in the morning; after that she took over the ward. She dug recipes out of the huge Jamaican girl; she made everyone talk about their jobs or husbands or families; the nurses found themselves crossly reminding her that she had been dying two days before. Her visitors were extraordinary; one, a leek-like, limp young man, had an expression of permanent woe which concealed (she assured us) a colossal self-confidence. She made him bring in a bottle of wine – a diluted rosé of non-French extraction. She offered it round when only the Spanish nurse was watching; it was the beginning of the end.

Towards the end of the week my mother, rushing in like a bird late back to the nest, deplored the fact that I was not in a private room; but by that time I knew better. I had realized what an enormous protection the ward can be against the glooms and nightmares of hospital – provided, of course, that it is a decent ward. We were lucky; there were only eight of us; we had no chronic old women wetting and wheezing in the night; the staff were scrupulous about drawing our cubicle curtains before attending to our more indecent needs.

There were two great advantages. The constant trivial conversation, the feeling that we were all in the same boat, provided a great bulwark against the blues; and the presence of other people helped to counteract one of the most maddening things about hospital – the fact that you never know what the hell is going on. By keeping our wits about us and pooling our information, we could realize that if they tried to give one the same injection twice in an hour it was probably a mistake, or how long they were likely to keep you on a given type of pill. We developed our own language of euphemism: 'going upstairs' meant the cleaning up operation which preceded release from hospital; 'losing' meant what it did to the woman in the Bible – and raised a laugh when the young house surgeon said 'How are you keeping?' and the answer was 'I'm not – I'm losing'.

True, in a private ward one could have telephoned or been visited by one's friends; but I doubt if one would have been up to it. The real world, after all, does not provide conversations that you can go to sleep in the middle of without giving offence; nor can you talk to your friends, day in, day out, like the doctor's column of a woman's magazine.

Gynaecology, there's no getting away from it, is a great leveller. Men have football and sex and cars to talk about to all other men without distinction; but there can be nothing as universal as obstetrics, even in its most preliminary forms. One was conscious of the common lot of women, of an overriding interest in the problem which, oddly enough, knocked down the barriers even between those who had wanted their babies and those who had not. One girl was in following an attempt – incredibly, a successful attempt – done with a syringe at four and a half months; she shared the same

61

sympathy, and the only person who was nasty to her was the female doctor.

The girl who set the tone for a lot of this was a demure little clerk who, at twenty-four, had had the same job for seven years: she was allowed to walk about and she would trot round doing the flowers or wheeling the telephone from bed to bed; her rather laborious kindness was as comforting as tea. One may have realized, in a dim way, that in real life she would probably be both prissy and dull; there, we were grateful, and accepted her as a leader.

Her husband was thickset and patient and wore a blazer; he would have been the admirable sixth or seventh bat of any cricket team, his wildest moment at a bar with beer. They suited each other perfectly.

In fact it was extraordinary, almost enough to make one believe in women's magazines, how well the women did match their men. The sweet Irish thirty-year-old, with two children already and an enormous misty regret about her miscarriage, had a comparably nice husband, Irish, moderately attractive, kind with the flowers and messages. There was one girl, like a blonde kitten, with the most raucous Cockney laugh I ever heard but incredible charm, who was always bouncing in and out of bed when she shouldn't, whose husband was like Seth in *Cold Comfort Farm*: he had side-whiskers and a Brando walk. The two of them exuded sex; the throbbing attraction that held them together was almost embarrassing; but there was a sort of childishness about them both that made everyone smile maternally – even when he came and hauled her out of hospital two days too soon, as he was sick of coping with the children.

The week went on; we got better; the nurses dropped in to smoke and forgot to take our blood-pressure. We got up, and padded into the sooty gardens in our dressing-gowns, conversing with the enormous hospital cat who lived there. This animal had recently broken a leg; the entire resources of the hospital being apparently insufficient to splint it, they had called in a vet; there was a bill for a fiver. At this point the hospital realized that there was absolutely nowhere in their accounts that they could write down 'To repairing cat – £5' and a rather sheepish notice went up on the noticeboard to demand – and get – the sum by popular subscription.

One by one, we Went Upstairs, came down in various states of grogginess, hiccups or tears; one demanded her husband's roses and woke up to find them laid funereally across her chest. We built up grievances, hugging ourselves when we could say 'We missed our cup of tea!' in tones of fury. Visiting hours became more riotous, but after them we suffered the grey, whining depression of convalescence; the outer world was coming too close.

But about this time I got sent a hamper. It was the kind of hamper that crops up in Victorian stories about the relief of poor families: it had fresh peaches and pâté and real turtle soup and eau-de-cologne. That evening we received our visitors in a haze of eau-de-cologne, and after they had gone we had caviare. Half of us hated it, of course – but we adored the *idea* of having caviare in hospital (and actually giving caviare to the general is a pleasure Horatio never thought of). We passed round two bottles of smuggled Sauternes; we pattered about in bare feet; we behaved as if it was an end-of-term feast in the dorm.

It was bad luck that it was Old Stuff-Shirt who wheeled round our tray of pills in the middle of it. 'Drinking,' she said in a voice which turned the wine to methylated in our mouths. 'In hospital!' She made us feel like old bawdy females in Newgate Prison. I remembered that in France I'd had wine two days after I'd lost my appendix; someone tried to explain that there was iron in wine. 'There is not,' she said firmly. 'Well, you can't have sleeping-pills with alcohol inside you.'

63

15 · *Any Answers?*

Few of our advice columns have to cope with the problem of a man whose wife not only bites him but has her teeth sharpened by tribal custom; nor do their bromides on husband-wife relationships generally have to take into account more than one legal wife.

*Tell me, Josephine,** a book based on a column in the *Central African Mail*, takes such things in its stride; but it is not just the variety of situation, it is also the humanity and humour that make one want, after reading it, to adapt Lincoln's phrase; and say to *Woman* and *Woman's Own*: 'The world is larger than your lonelyheart, madam.'

Josephine has to sort out people who are in debt to their witch-doctors, or whose tribal elders have arranged unwelcome marriages for them, sight unseen; she copes not only with men who cannot pay a bride-price, but with men who have the money but no means of converting it into the necessary cows.

She deals with a girl who has been living with the father of her child for years, but cannot marry him because she is Catholic and he is London Missionary Society; and with a student who shares an electric light bulb with a neighbour who wants lights out at nine.

The advice is refreshingly practical: the student should get an oil-lamp, the bitten man must either get a divorce and let his wife bite someone else or find a way of keeping her off the beer. And, presumably because there are so many codes

---

* *Tell me, Josephine*, edited by Barbara Hall (André Deutsch, 15s).

jostling together, there is a splendid absence of moral high-handedness.

The Josephine column caters entirely for Africans; and it is perhaps no coincidence that the only one to rival it in gusto is the *Dear Maisie* column in *Flamingo*, a magazine for West Indians and Africans in London.

'What makes you think *any* man actually wants to get married?' demands Maisie of an overscrupulous girl. 'Stop trying to be fair – act like a woman.' To a girl whose English boyfriend keeps eyeing other girls, she says: 'Well, at least it shows he's normal. Judging from some Englishmen you meet, that's good.'

To a man who is afraid that his girl's excessive demands will weaken his career ('I did hear that a previous lover of this girl died from exhaustion'), she says: 'You poor old thing. Actually you sound too feeble to have much of a career ahead of you anyway.'

The snag, of course, of avoiding so completely the treacle-filled pitfall of such columns is that you can end up in the other one, which is filled with grit; the special haunt of Abby van Buren, the best-known Miss Lonelyhearts in America. When a problem really can be answered in a sentence, Dear Abby is superb: to the mother-in-law who worried whether a nine-pound baby could really be premature, she replied: 'The baby was on time. The wedding was late. Forget it.' But she is also capable of brushing off serious problems with a facetious crack: to the woman who lived in want because her husband kept saving for a rainy day, she simply says: 'Tell him it's raining' – and a fat lot of use *that* is. The *Mirror* group's Marjorie Proops, shrewdest and wittiest of our native products, has the edge on Dear Abby, if only because she has the sense not to tackle in a short answer a problem that can only be done properly at length.

The Courrier du Cœur in *Elle* gives longer answers, and

is, to my mind, the only one in the Northern Hemisphere that one can imagine a sensible person actually going to for serious advice. Marcelle Segal's great strength is her feeling for the complexities. 'You will be happy,' she tells one woman, 'not perfectly, but relatively – as all happy people are happy.' 'You took the easy way out (moving in with in-laws) and like all who look for the easy way, you found it led to appalling difficulties.'

She can also be pretty caustic, as when she told a woman who complained that her handsome bridegroom watched TV instead of chatting her up, that as she had married him for his looks and not his conversation, she could hardly grumble.

Given that question, a British magazine would almost certainly have told her to 'have a talk with her husband', which remains their favourite advice – though in most cases if the couple had been able to talk to each other the problem would never have arisen at all.

Their other two standard recommendations are to join a club, if you are lonely, and to say 'No' if you are not: in fact, the frequency with which they say that 'one shouldn't yield to temptation' makes one want to answer, as in *The Dolly Dialogues*: 'Well, someone must or the thing becomes absurd.'

But what is really wrong with our advice columns is not that they are written from a standard moral viewpoint: one can just imagine the uproar there would be if they were not. It is not that their ideal is a conventionally happy marriage with two clean children and a well-kept house; it is that they seem to have nothing to say to the vast number of people whose troubles never come anywhere near this neat little semi-det. of the emotions.

Anyone whose ear is bent by their own friends' troubles hears more variety of gloom in a week than these people seem to handle in a year; it is inconceivable that, with fifteen million readers between them, they really hear of only ten types of trouble (at least six liable to end up with the Council for the Unmarried Mother).

People are frigid, obsessed, queer; people get lonely; they get into the wrong jobs and married to the wrong people; like John Grubby, they worry because they are short and stout and/or troubled by religious doubt. But one looks in vain for any sign of this in the magazines; any suggestion that one can be a stronger person for being unhappy, that even a disastrous love can stretch the muscles of the spirit, that we are all poor bastards who have to make the best of things somehow. With cruel optimism they advise people to write off their imperfect relationships, on the assumption that perfect ones will follow. But why should they?

I remember a week in which the main lovelorn letter in *Woman's Own* was from a woman who, married to a widower older than herself, had fallen in love with his son. The reply was characteristic: 'Gillian is only adding to her worries by trying to convince herself that what she feels is more than infatuation. . . . I think Gillian and her husband should entertain more younger couples . . . she may be missing young companions' – and so on. To get the measure of this sort of advice, you need do only one thing. Cross out the name 'Gillian' and write in 'Phèdre.'

16 · It's All My Own Work

Lying in my bath the other day listening to the sound of someone else peeling the potatoes I reflected how delightful it is to have someone else do your work for you, how bearable it is to do it yourself, and how absolutely intolerable it is to be 'helped'.

In fact leaping into a bath as soon as anyone does offer to do anything is about the only way of preventing them doubling the amount *you* have to do.

There are the helpers who create work from nothing – the ones who go around disturbing dirty cups that were perfectly all right where they were, or who smugly announce they have ironed the non-iron shirt. There are the forestallers, on whose account you have to wash up every pan without leaving it to soak: their only sadness is that they cannot sneak up in the morning and make the beds before anyone is up.

There are the expert finishers, who sprinkle chives on your soup, decorate your cakes and fold the nappies you have laboriously washed, thus removing that all-my-own-work feeling when the hard slog is over. And there are the keen participators who insist on helping you with the job you are actually at, emptying water jugs into your washing-up water, or cracking their skulls on yours as they leap up to pass you the salt. And all the time you long to slap their hands away, you have to go on saying thank you, thank you, thank you.

Of course there are helpers who can take on a bit of work without driving one to distraction. There is the comfortable friend who will sit smoking at the kitchen table until you dump a lump of cheese and a grater in front of her – friends are better at this than relations because they are mostly lazier. There is the utterly reliable person who will take over a job regularly – I have even heard that some husbands empty buckets on this basis.

Really subordinate help, that you can order about, is fine – only generally this has to be paid help. The only people who have ever successfully welded their relations into an efficient work force were those hideous old Chinese grandmothers who shrewdly worked on a basis of absolute tyranny.

But good help of any kind is rare. And the silliest thing about it all is that the helpers are undoubtedly hating it quite as much as the helped – one only has to remember, in one's teens, the almighty drag of 'helping your mother' compared to the thrill of being allowed to make the dinner.

So often, of course, the thing that makes help impossible is simply that two incompatible systems meet head on. I can make a mayonnaise, but not on my hostess's cute machine; my mother-in-law can chop herbs like an Italian cutting hair, but not in my folksy little herb cutter.

One family has a tradition that the washing-up is done directly a meal is over, but not in any circumstances by the woman who has just cooked it; in another the cook does wash up, but only when and if she feels like it; the great thing to be said for washing up before a meal instead of after being that you at least have the incentive of hunger. Both traditions are humane enough; but when the two families meet, the wretched cook is forced to the sink by pressure of public opinion before she has barely begun to digest.

In household drudgery, the feeling of a single job well completed is about the only satisfaction one gets. But I am not sure that the principle of one bod – one job is not pretty important in shops and offices, too. If you give a man a job to do, some simple little task like programming a computer or mending your shoes or bringing down the Government, he will do it; taking the maximum pride in a job for which he will be praised and paid. Or he will not do it; in which case it will at least be clear under which trouser-seat the fire should be lit.

But once you get several people helping each other ('advising' is the office word for this), several things follow. A man will not, for a start, work so hard: just as guest ironers always leave one table mat at the bottom of the bag, so no one is going to stay till ten to complete a job someone else will, in any case, finish tomorrow. He will constantly feel someone else is getting the credit, even if the someone is, in fact, carrying the can; and if he is totally incompetent it may be months, if not years, before it becomes clear whose spanner was jamming the works.

Eliot Jaques has a theory that people should get paid according to the length of time that elapses before their mistakes are checked – ten minutes for a factory hand, three weeks for a foreman and a couple of years for a manager. But if you get a sufficiently confused chain of command it may never be clear who went wrong.

I once worked for a man who thought it amusing to have two people doing every job; the result was that we spent a third of our time trying to grab the work before the other one did, another third explaining why the other had got there first and only a third actually working. It made me wonder whether those apparently absurd Union disputes where the Carpenter brings out his union if a Boilermaker bangs a nail are prompted not so much by injured pride as by a lively fear that, without clear demarcation, he will find somebody else's helpful hammer descending on his thumb.

Reactionary as it sounds, I think that at a personal level democracy – by which I mean a dozen people of equal status standing on each other's shoe-laces – does not work. Everyone needs to be solely in charge of their own little bit of business, if it is only marshalling the paper-clips: justice consists of being held responsible for only your own work; of having access to the man above your own boss. Co-operation becomes simply a state in which pride and responsibility disappear, unless it is absolutely clear who does what. Even the Army, heaven knows a cumbersome piece of machinery, has worked out a chain of command such that no general is going to be helped to win a battle.

We all know that too many cooks spoil the broth, but this is not just because three will remember the pepper and none the salt; or because they will crash into each other's ladles as they plunge about the kitchen; or even because one will quite sincerely suppose artichoke when the plan was for mulligatawny. It is because no one cook is going to be praised for it personally, or blamed if the stuff tastes awful: which, in the circumstances, it almost certainly will.

17 · As Rich as You Feel

Few people in their own eyes are rich or poor: they are all ordinary. This, when I was doing fashion, used to be one of the things that made advising people difficult: the woman who thought thirty pounds was the right price for a suit considered herself just as 'typical' as the woman who paid twelve.

Indeed as far as I can see the only people who ever have any positive consciousness of their own wealth are those who have come by it suddenly; and it is interesting to see the precise moment at which they realized they were not hard up any longer.

One man said it was the first time he rode in a taxi without watching the clock, for another it was the first time he left his car too long on a parking-meter on purpose. One journalist said it was having two drinks to offer people instead of one take-it-or-leave-it bottle of bad sherry; another that it was not going to the hairdresser because she had no time, instead of no money.

Monica Furlong said it was the joy of being able to pay bills on time; Julian More said it was being reconnected quickly when the telephone had been cut off for non-payment. Paul McCartney realized what had happened to him when he found himself giving a taxi-driver a ten-bob tip.

Clothes come into it: there was the fashion buyer who ruined a pair of four-guinea gloves, and realized she could buy others, that it was not the end of the world; there was a reader whose windfall made her suddenly realize she did not have to have *any* nasty clothes; one man said prosperity meant two clean shirts a day without thinking about it, and another said it was throwing away socks with holes in them instead of just going on wearing them.

When you ask people who are not rich what coming into money would mean to them, you get equally curious answers. They all start out half-heartedly listing the conventional yacht, pent-house, peerage, but their eyes light up only when they get down to cases and add: 'And a carpet in the bathroom!' 'Wine every meal!' 'Not having to keep the string off parcels.'

A man would not go first class if he was Charlie Clore but longs to be able to go abroad without notice, instead of planning for months to get his money's worth out of the fare. One woman would hardly buy a single new dress, but dreams of a proper cupboard to hang things in.

What I cannot help wondering is whether one could not perfectly well achieve at least some of these Midas symbols without getting rich at all. Some people, indeed, seem to manage it. The man who lives in a decrepit cabin with a Cadillac at the door, or the Chelsea writer whose jersey has not been changed since the first Labour Government but who always seems to have the price of a gallon of petrol or wine; the bespectacled youth from the outer suburbs who shyly confesses to a £500 camera: all these have obviously grasped the fact that you can afford what you want amazingly often so long as you never waste a penny on what other people think you ought to want.

I know a man who, in a noble rage, went out and bought a lifetime's supply of carbon paper because he was sick of economizing on the stuff, and now feels that Rockefeller has nothing on him; my spy in Slough says there is a man there who has built behind his modest dwelling a swimming-pool so vast that it obliterates his entire back garden. He cannot be the only man in Bucks who prefers swimming to mowing

74

the lawn; he is just the only one who has carried the thing through.

What is wanted is a policy of highly selective extravagance. It sounds expensive to buy a new battery every winter for your car and pay a boy to wash it – but if a clean car that goes is all you want, it comes out a lot cheaper than buying a new car. Or take the fuss we had some time ago in the *Observer* about the heated lavatory seat. The purists pointed out that with a properly heated house you don't need one – and it is true that nowhere but in Britain are there so many heated pads and muffs and lamps – and that, moreover, the thing was ridiculously expensive. But the point is that if there is only one place where the cold catches you bending it makes better sense to pay far too much for a heated seat than the right price – which is hundreds of pounds – for a heated house.

Those of us who never are going to win the pools can console ourselves, grudgingly, with the thought that having pots and pots of money might not be all simple ecstasy anyway. Pools winners are often reported as being miserable in a matter of months: only the ones who really wanted to break out completely make a go of it. The others wanted new curtains or new teeth or new fridges; what they got was new lives, which they did not want. I have no idea whether it is true (as their masseuses say) that some of the really rich suffer from crippling fits of meanness; whether they really are as laughably convinced of their own poverty as some of them say they are; whether they are as unable to stop knowing one another as they appear (I once asked a nice rich man why he liked a certain hag-like rich woman, and got the answer, 'I don't *like* her – it's just that she invites us . . . we invite her. . . .'). But whatever life up there is like, one can assume it has its own set of problems and stresses. What most of us really want is to pick one or two of the golden apples and get clean away.

'Come on boys,' says someone in P. G. Wodehouse's memoirs, 'Flo Ziegfeld is feeling rich today.'

'Flo always does,' someone answered gloomily, 'the trouble is, it's just a feeling.'

It is, after all, the feeling that counts.

18 · The Kitchen Think

It is some time now since Peg Bracken provoked a sigh of relief that could be heard clear across the Atlantic with her *I Hate to Cook Book*, and followed it up with one on Hating to Housekeep: the books being designed to cheer along the woman who is forced to go through the motions of cooking and homemaking without having any natural aptitude for either. It seems to me it is about time someone broke in on the market with something that would fill an even longer felt want: the *I Hate to Think Book*.

The Bracken method depends on facing up honestly to your unwillingness to do the chore, and then concentrating unashamedly on the short cuts. And there are short cuts in plenty for those who hate to think. There is, for example, the equivalent of hay-box cookery, of casserole cookery, or Getting It All Done the Day Before: you resign yourself to actually doing a little thinking, when you are twenty-one or so, and then making it last. Having discovered by concentration or independent experiment that atheism does not work or nylon is non-porous or means tests are unfair, you fasten your mind with a snap and take the thought out all ready just before it is needed, thus avoiding any last-minute rush.

Nowhere can this more easily be done than in the treatment of Abroad. One does not need to be so obvious as Nancy Mitford's Uncle Matt, who stated that abroad was bloody and all foreigners fiends; you simply need one broadside per country designed to ward off any foreign influences trying to land.

The social justice of the Swedes, for example, can be written off by tirelessly reminding the company that they have the highest suicide rate in the world – actually, they come eighth, but you need not bother with a little thing like that. Again, if anyone suggests that Frenchwomen fuss about their food more effectively than their English equivalents, you point out that foreigners muck about disguising everything with sauces because their materials are inferior. The most cursory glance at the history of French cooking shows that it came to flower in the Touraine, where the materials are superb, but with any luck your audience will just nod sagely.

You can dispose of all Americans with the crack about their going from barbarism to decadence with no intervening period of civilization, dismiss the Swiss with Harry Lime's phrase about the cuckoo-clock and generally lighten (as with egg white) all conversation about abroad by quoting the remark about foreigners understanding English spoken *very loud* as if it was (a) funny and (b) your own invention.

The production of standard phrases need not, of course, be confined to comments on foreigners – there are certain pre-packaged remarks which are happily consumed by families all over the country. But a word of warning here. Just as Peg Bracken says it is a mistake to serve a stand-by dish so often that the family get sick of it, so there is a slight danger that the very frequency of its repetition may alert your audience to the unthought involved.

For example, it occurred to me to take a second look at that remark about the Royal Family not being able to answer back – sounds quite sensible the first time you hear it; it is only the thirty-second time you hear it repeated in exactly the same words that you realize that it is nonsense. There is nothing in the Constitution to stop them, they have simply realized (and they are not the only ones) that in the long run silence works better than retorts. Wise they may be not to answer back: but holding your fire is not the same as being unarmed.

The woman who hates to housekeep disposes of a lot by simply slamming doors on the chaos, and the woman – or man for that matter – who hates to think can use much the same technique. Such doors are 'I may be old-fashioned but . . .' since being out of date is so closely linked to soundness in the British mind; or 'I always think . . .' – if you've always thought it, no one will be able to bring themselves to disturb you now; and all those sentences that begin 'I wouldn't like *my* wife/baby/secretary' and go on 'to work/ wear plastic pants/use a Dictaphone' thus neatly by-passing any actual discussion of the issues involved.

Much, too, can be done with phrases such as 'reliable brand name' and 'old-established concern'; and it is only rarely that the rug is pulled from under you by events, like the poor man who said 'After all, he is a Minister of the Crown' at the beginning of the Profumo scandals.

The great thing to remember is that we live in an age of TV, radio, headlines, posters and commentators, and that with prepackaged thought so readily available, you need refuse to talk, even if you have no time for the traditional preparation.

19 · The Bore Lords

Whenever you see a woman going into a cinema where they are showing a war film, you know that whatever war it is about one battle has been lost already: her struggle to get taken to something that has any chance of interesting her.

And once inside, she cannot escape: all those bazookas, all those cheery barrack scenes where they can't use the Army's only adjective; all those exploding piles of earth and planes that sweep from the left of the sky to the right and then (by reversing the film) from the right to the left; the scene where the Marine finds his manhood in Malaya. I suppose all these films do have different scripts and use the same noises-off only in parts; but I imagine I am not the only female for whom they have all long since fused into one indistinguishable and interminable yawn.

In the cinema you are trapped; with the printed word things are easier: you can simply turn over. And this year, with two war anniversaries, has been a particularly propitious one for getting through a paper in less time than it takes to read it. You can hardly open one of them without someone's reconstruction of why some military exercise happened or didn't happen or should have happened; some general or war correspondent living it all again, some historian or Chelsea pensioner trying to drag us back by the hair to the times when the things men enjoy (such as guns and all-male camaraderie) were dominant, because they had to be; and female pre-occupations (such as cooking and having your man around) were at an all-time low.

Until now I have always felt guilty about skipping all this:

I probably ought to read them, I thought, as a part of seeing that it doesn't happen again, or facing up to reality or some such thing.

But it has suddenly struck me that the men aren't going through all this from a sense of duty. All these characters who pore over old battle plans and get worked up over the operation of guns, who race down at dawn to pluck the magazines from the mat, are being no more conscientious than I am; editors, after all, are a good deal too shrewd to sell their papers on the basis of what people *ought* to read. No: men *like* it. Whatever their feelings about violence or politics or the morality of war, the mechanics of battle delight them: men actually, heaven help us, find it fun.

This applies just as much, of course, to such present wars as can be scraped together; news editors anywhere are apt to put the most minuscule war on the front page. The alleged reason is that since people are getting killed, this is serious; and that any war, however piffling, might grow into a big war that will blow us all up. But I doubt it. Thousands more die daily from starvation without making the front page, and everybody knows that a jungle skirmish is turned into an atom war in Moscow or Washington or Peking, not because of four miles of undergrowth captured either way. A report on a minor war in the antipodes will drive out a childcare feature any day; but not because the war is more important: simply because fighting exercises exactly the same sort of primeval fascination for men that children do for women.

It would be agreeable if, flushed with high moral fervour about wars and men, I could represent women as a force for peace. Unfortunately we are just as good at the emotions which lead to wars, such as greed and intolerance and too much national pride; and conscientious objectors say that when it comes to making their lives hell women are worse than men.

But I do think that to women the idea of grown people actually killing one another – I mean killing people you don't even *know* – seems more senseless; and we have less interest in the mechanisms of killing because they seem either quite unreal, like little boys going 'bang-bang – you're dead'; or deadly in earnest, in which case they are much too terrifying to enjoy thinking about.

Women have their reservations, too, about the sanctity of things military, of the ease with which defence expenditure gets sanctioned compared with any other – compare the £350 million we spend on conventional forces overseas with the £175 million that goes to underdeveloped countries.

Again, while even unwarlike men often think a service training is good for the character, women are less convinced about military virtues. Courage and decision may be fine, but absolute obedience to authority is a hell of a quality for ordinary life; likewise the assumption that the job must always come first and the family second; likewise the nailing down of the nerves against one's horror at blood and screams and suffering.

For all that, we have always had a certain uneasiness about attacking the military ethos: come wartime, we feel, and we may be only too glad of qualities which seem senseless in peacetime. And we still have an atavistic fear of the vile but undeniable link between men and power and guns: the feeling that men might not be altogether men if they were not demonstrably strong. In any case, our attempts to breed out the military impulse are apt to fail: the fact that I cannot straighten up anywhere in our attic flat without knocking down two Colts and a Mauser is the direct result of my husband's peace-loving parents having denied him guns as a child.

The atom may be making the skills of these earlier wars as outdated as the crossbow; there may even be a certain danger in anything that encourages people to think that wars can any longer be won. More likely the game is harmless enough – but the realization that all this war-lore is just a male hobby might make us less shamefaced about our boredom with it all. For the one thing it is not is grimly realistic. Robert E. Lee said that it was just as well war was so horrible or men would love it too much; and no one who was thinking of the horror could really find it such excellent entertainment.

20 · A Surfeit of Diets

It is a truth universally acknowledged that all winter clothes shrink two inches round the hips in the course of the summer. And for those who do not propose to get a complete new wardrobe September is a grim month.

Women stop other women in the street vainly asking for a painless way to knock off the pounds, while diets spread and fade round a neighbourhood like epidemics in the spring term.

Those who keep their ears and eyes open on the subject learn startling things. One man who got hooked on Limmitts slimming biscuits couldn't stop eating them even at meals. Another lost weight on huge meals of spaghetti, between which he rowed himself round and round the Bay of Naples.

An Information officer of the C.B.I. once took up a diet that sliced two-and-a-half stone off him in three months: low in carbohydrate, its distinguishing features were a dose of salts and hot lemon-juice in the early dawn, a squalid tin of raisins carried round to parties as a charm against the dreaded canapé, and – get this – unrestricted whisky.

Another plan that calls for no teetotalism is the Unfatted Metcalf diet: John Metcalf's philosophy being, he says, to stupefy the stomach. This organ, he reasons, is trained by habit to send up messages of alarm and despondency at given intervals: give the thing a nervous breakdown by feeding it prodigiously one minute and starving it the next, and it will give up sending messages altogether. Any meals he doesn't have to eat, he misses out completely; but when he does eat, he eats like a human being and not like a finicky sparrow.

Again, I have known people put their faith most effectively in diets based on the fallacy of liquid retention (unless you've actually got dropsy, or are retaining it for gynaecological reasons, liquid makes no difference). The reason the diets worked was mainly that they were set by an ogre whom they dared not face with their weight undiminished.

The most bizarre diet I know is the plan of the woman who simply 'thinks slim' – which means simply becoming aware of how much she eats: an appalling revelation. Inflamed by these accounts, I am thinking of trying the Spock Special: if urging food on someone really does destroy the appetite as he suggests, obviously I ought to sit in a highchair and get someone to feed me too much too often with a huge spoon.

All these diets are, admittedly, absurd. But I have noticed an odd thing in journalism: that the sensible journalists, who know perfectly well that only high-protein, low-carbohydrate diets can possibly work, are appreciably fatter than the flossies on the glossies who pursue each mad banting fashion as it comes along, eating groats and gin one month or spinach and high-octane petrol the next. Why? Because the thing that really counts is the incentive.

Sometimes it is simply the initial spur that does the trick. A masseuse saying, 'Were you ever slim?', a viewer writing in to say how awful one looks on television, some comforting (he thinks) boyfriend saying he *likes* plump girls – all these help; but there is absolutely nothing to beat a simple tour of the dress shops for sending you screaming back to the non-stick frying-pan and the sawdust rolls.

People give things up for Lent as a sign of religious conviction, but for really staying away from the fleshpots vanity wins every time.

Those of us who long ago realized that we cannot both eat what we like and wear what we like without periodic blitzes, have discovered certain principles which seem important with almost any diet. First, don't try to mix two at once. A girl who says on the one hand, 'Any amount of protein is O.K.' and then, with a slab of steak inside her, switches to 'A slice of bread and butter is only 100 calories' will lose nothing but her waistline. Second, stick to the diet for a week *after* you have got down to par: if you leap up with a glad cry and eat fifty potatoes the moment the needle touches zero you may find yourself back at the beginning again.

You should resist, too, the temptation to reward yourself for your abstentions, as the reward tends to outweigh the abstinence – a fact pointed out to me last week by a man who was at that moment eating the piece of sugar he hadn't had in his coffee.

And if there is one time of day when you have no resistance, it pays to allow for it: I have a sort of kitchen curfew under which anything not locked up by 11 p.m. gets eaten, so I have to arrive at that point with a hundred calories in hand.

Finally you have to distinguish between crash diets and maintaining diets. Trying to make a lifelong union out of a crash diet is as dangerous as an affair with a long-term diet is disappointing.

A crash programme often works *better* if you hate the food – you are sustained by virtuous fervour like Luther at the Diet of Worms; but a diet you are going to stick with had better be one you like. Theodora Fitzgibbon's *High Protein Diet and Cookery Book* is a great help here, not only for the recipes but for the principles: for example the idea of doing casseroles by browning only the meat, pouring off the excess fat and thickening with an egg-yolk instead of flour.

By the same token, don't be too sure you have to give up alcohol. A small drink can often decide you against a large meal, or even make you forget you haven't had it.

86

We all know how to eat sensibly, just as we all know how to be good: the trouble is getting down to it. To those who are resigned to dieting off and on forever the nonsense takes away some of the tedium. We can say, like Pooh Bear, that it doesn't really matter, if I don't get any fatter, and I *don't* get any fatter – what I do. And to those who are not resigned – well, at the time of the Battle of Trafalgar, Lady Hamilton weighed thirteen stone.

21 · *The Grammarian's Funeral*

The letters that journalists dread most are not the ones that accuse one of being a Fascist beast or a Communist stooge; not the ones that tirelessly exhort you to say Cellophane not cellophane, Thermos not thermos; nor even the ones that urge you to address all six members of the Outer Hebrides Wee Free Crofters' Luncheon Club no expenses paid.

They are the ones which accuse us of using the tools of our trade wrongly – the ones that point out our grammatical mistakes.

I certainly hang my head in shame when they say I don't know the difference between militate and mitigate, or between blaming him for the murder and blaming the murder on him. But having recently been absurdly rebuked for using the 'meaningless' phrase *chatting up*, I am beginning to wonder if these letter-writers, these guardians of the purity of the English language, are not slightly in the position of a cavalier risking his life and reputation defending the virginity of Nell Gwyn. Have they, one asks oneself, perhaps missed the point altogether?

We all have bits of bad English about which we feel smugly knowledgeable. I hate aggravate instead of irritate, people who mix up infer and imply, and anyone who puts 'the' in front of 'hoi polloi'; I have bopped many a secretary for writing 'alright' or writing 'it's' in a sentence such as 'The cat drinks its milk' as if the cat had staggered back exclaiming: 'It's milk!'

I don't say centre round and I don't say under the circumstances, and it sets my teeth on edge when people do; my

88

contortions to avoid a split infinitive are such that my right foot often ends up inextricably wedged in my left armpit. But I am beginning to think that one winces as instinctively and with as little real sense at all this as one does when a chalk squeaks across a blackboard.

Take, for example, this phrase 'chatting up' – and with it two more which make English adrenalin flow like water: 'washing up' (in the American sense) and the phrase 'literary-type student': all three depending on the use of prepositions.

When an American man goes off to wash up this is not because a man's work is never done, but simply because he has gritty fingernails: and using the preposition this way robs it of its transitive English-English meaning, to wash up something else. So I guess (disgusting!) reckon (how slangy can you get?) – I *suppose* that we are right to resist this Americanization.

But 'chatting up' also has this transitive implication – quite different from chatting, the phrase means chatting with a purpose, whether to please or cheat. I cannot really defend my hatred of the phrase 'literary-type': the literary-type student is the kind you meet at literary parties; not a literary student who is at home writing books. If it is just as clear as 'literary type *of* student' (and it is) what did we need that preposition for anyway?

Very often, all that is happening in these linguistic battles is that spoken English is changing into written. The American use of 'theme' for 'essay' and 'formula' for 'bottle-of-milk-mixture' obviously comes from speech. 'What's the theme this week?' they ask, or 'Do you use sugar in your formula?' I hate it, but taking the part for the whole is good old English usage, and no more lacking in moral fibre than 'all hands on deck'.

And you only have to teach English to foreigners to realize how far from spoken English 'correct' English actually is. I came on a whole community of Finns diligently saying, 'I shall go for aye walk,' and worrying in case they should have said 'will'; it sounded absurd because no Englishman ever *says* 'shall' – he says 'I'll go furra walk,' thus bypassing the agony of will *v.* shall altogether. I don't know why we don't write it the way we say it.

The late A. P. Rossiter, who cared passionately about language, did a lot to point out the difference between the two, citing the classic instance of the man giving a Third Programme talk under heads (1), (2), (3), and (4) who actually said 'see (4) above'. But he was the first to realize that airscript – English written to sound as if you were saying it – was not just tape-recorded speech. For one thing, real speech is too diffuse: you can say twice as much in a prepared script of 500 words as you can in four minutes of random speech at 130 words a minute – which is one of the reasons television interviews manage to say so little.

But it is, for all that, from the rhythms and immediacy of speech that the written language is constantly revived; and one cannot hold out indefinitely for a sort of Mandarin *Times*ese. Grammar is vital, even for simple clarity; but grammar becomes eroded with time: Finnish, with its fifteen cases, is a primitive and inflexible language compared to American, which is, in its turn, a good deal simpler than English.

Nor am I trying to produce a sort of Wordsworthian worship of common speech, meaning whatever common people say: what they say is only too often a copy of a very bad film with a written script. But the further away from speaking you go, the harder good language becomes: there are three people who can speak well for every one that can write a decent letter, three who can write letters for every one who can do journalism, and three who can do journalism for every one who writes good books.

There is no way of stopping one's nerves clashing together like wires if someone says 'like wires do' – but there is no valid reason why you shouldn't use 'like' with a verb: it is only habit that makes us hate it. And 'contact' has as good a right to grow up into a verb as any other noun – at least it is neater than 'make contact with' and less absurd than 'get in touch with'. In clothes, the informal always replaces the formal – men's tails were once casual riding wear, their town suits the lounging suits of country gentlemen. And the same is true of language. Even as a bird out of Fowler's snare, it escapes away and is set free, and our attempts to fasten it down are either useless or fatal.

Look at the French, and their Academy, and those poor old men wringing their hands to prevent slang joining the Jockey Club – and what happens? – they have more American words in their language than tourists on their beaches.

But if anyone thinks I am going to give over this aggravating intellectual-type stand, and say 'centres round' just like the hoi polloi do, they've got another think coming.

22 · *Surely You Taught Them Something?*

Angus Wilson's roughcast atheists, the darling Dodos, produced prissy R.C. offspring; girls from the rectory often feel a call to be call girls; tough pioneering parents are only too apt to produce layabout sons who play the horses.

Such is the power of reaction, in fact, that telling children what to think can often make them do the exact opposite.

As a beginner parent, I have noticed that there is a welter of instruction on how to give your child the right emotional, sexual, psychological start; and a fair amount about forming the teeth and strengthening the spine; but there is very little advice going on how to shape a child's mental attitudes.

What is missing is a sort of Socratic Spock; and in the absence of such a book I am appealing to readers to produce some substitute for it.

What about, for example, a right attitude to money? The easiest way to make sure a child never thinks money tells you anything about ability is the one employed by my father: of being visibly cleverer and poorer than anyone else – a schoolmaster. But if one is not, oneself, either harder up or higher minded than the neighbours, what can you do instead?

A firm system of pocket money can give a child a sense of its value, no doubt, but will not necessarily stop him being the sort of skinflint who would rather save for a rainy day than buy a month in the sun. More: if you keep a child too tight, might he not merely envy his free-fisted friends? Unless, of course, you can reinforce the policy with a lot of scorn for anyone whose money *shows*: an equally inadequate attitude.

Money wrapped up by a couple of generations gets called breeding and taste and a sense of quality and so forth; but it doesn't leave a man any more able to do without it. And being able to do without it is the one sure guarantee that he will never choose the wrong job or the wrong marriage because of the money.

There is, too, the allied problem of comfort. Most people of my generation were forced into a number of things that were Good for us, like eating up our fat and taking cold baths (pretending to take cold baths anyway). It is easy enough to say 'No child of mine shall ever be so cold he has to dress under the bedclothes!' But if you give him comfort from the word go will you not, like the bride in the black nightdress, leave him nothing to look forward to? Comfort is, after all, a great consolation of age.

Will he not then notice comfort only negatively, so that the soft bed means nothing to him, while the tedding and the spreading of the straw for a bedding drives him frantic? And yet it seems a bit hard to turn off the heating for his room alone and sleep soft oneself while the boy snores on his character-forming plank. Maybe this is why people send their sons to boarding-schools: they want them to do their seven years' hard, but they just can't bear to watch. Still, it seems an extreme solution.

More important than money or comfort or quality is the question of his attitude to authority. I don't mean mine, as I stand over him with a cricket bat urging him to eat spinach, but impersonal authority, Government authority: the taxman and the policeman. Obviously, people who carve up railway carriages have too little respect for authority, and any modern State in which everyone resentfully cheats on their income tax and fiddles the Government contracts is simply inefficient.

But it is equally clear that too great a sense of orders being orders leads to a Prussian mulishness. I would rather hate to have a son who did *not* feel that, in P. G. Wodehouse's words, if more young men went around pushing policemen in the stomach the world would be a better and purer place.

I think perhaps the people who grew up through the very idealistic socialism of the thirties – or who were educated by them – found it easiest to get this one right. For them, the State was potentially the people's power against bullying big business, so they could see something like T.V.A. as *their* project; but as all the brighter sparks tended to get in trouble with the powers that were sooner or later, they had no illusions about the divine right of courts – or cops.

Authority ought to be the common repository of our sense of justice, our Sunday best thinking, as Matthew Arnold had it. And children have a very strong sense of justice – 'it's not *fair*!' is their constant wail. What happens to it later? The child-care books, worrying about jealousy, often tell parents not to get mixed up in children's fights; but I cannot help wondering if banging their heads together and telling them both to shut up *is* the way to teach them that authority can be fair.

One final thing. I am convinced that no one has a chance to do what he is cut out to do or be fully himself unless he is capable of being alone. Alone to read two books a day at seventeen, or climb hills with a sketchbook; to write a deathless novel in a lonely bedsit or the foreign service of the B.B.C.; to devour law reports or medical textbooks for a profession.

But just making a child *be* alone might make him only too avid for company: I did almost no work at Cambridge simply because, having enough friends for the first time, I was incapable of saying no to any jaunt they suggested. I do not know whether the art of being alone but not lonely is a source of strength or its result; but I do know I would like my son to master it.

Socrates said that virtue couldn't be taught, pointing as his main argument to the sons of virtuous men, who were obviously washouts. It is the grandson of virtuous men I am worried about; and if anyone can think of a way to slip a few good notions past his guard, I would like to hear about it. Surely *somebody* must have succeeded in teaching their children *something*?

23 · Or Perhaps Not

From about next January we are going to give up sneering, smoking and picking our teeth; we will no longer wrangle over who should have been to the bank, get up after ten or allow the cats on the bed: an austere régime of perfect truth and beauty will simply have to set in.

For the one thing that came out overwhelmingly from the many splendid letters I got about children's upbringing is that what really counts is the way parents behave and think themselves. No deceptions, no precepts, no training tricks ever work, they say; so this ghastly programme of reform seems to be the only answer.

For all that, the letters were immensely cheering. We hear so much about baffled parents and angry young offspring that this massed evidence of stable families, of parents who had produced children they liked and respected, was a delightful counterblast – even if it still left me with several doubts about the questions I had asked.

How to be alone was the most specific problem, and so the easiest solved. Generally, parents held that a child must be alone from the beginning, but have a good reason for it: books before bedtime, a box of assorted objects to paw through; plenty of things going on – such as painting and stamps and carpentry – that needed no other people. One parent had even cured an incorrigibly gregarious youngster by building him a tree-house that would take only one.

Money was a trickier question. Most people saw a 'right attitude' as the ability not so much to take it or leave it alone as to handle it wisely. For this they had several techniques:

always making the child pay back what it owes, discussing mortgages in front of it, giving the neighbourhood rate in pocket money and leaving the child free in spending it; thinking aloud while shopping (fun for the grocer). Several noted that an identical plan produced different results in different members of the family, and concluded that it was a matter of temperament; two, of the school that believes that the hand of the potter shapes the final clay, said it was all a matter of toilet training, though they did not make it clear which method had the Midas touch.

I realize that I was naïve to think that attitudes to authority could be considered apart from the psychology of parental authority. But I hope I will be forgiven if I still wonder whether it is not also inadequate to consider it only in psychological terms. I am prepared to be convinced (by these letters, if nothing else) that parents who bring up a child with love and sense have a good chance of seeing him adopt their own ideals: the adjusted child will mostly grow up to fit in to his parents' social order.

But whether he is *right* in doing so might rather depend on whether the parents are Chinese Communists or Scottish Presbyterians or white South Africans; Cianos or Cecils or Kennedys. And if the children grow up to think for themselves (an ability all these parents valued highly) they will presumably be able to have ideas of what they think is a just society. One's idea of that depends on what one considers to be the True End of Man: on which any psychologist may have an opinion, but will have it *as* a man and not as an expert.

Behind the very confidence and tolerance these parents offer their children is, though I don't suppose they particularly think of it this way, an assumption about the basic soundness of human beings; as optimistic in its way as Adam Smith's confidence in the Hidden Hand guiding the trade cycle. Imagine Lord Chesterfield or a Spartan mother or an early Jesuit thinking all you had to do was clear the soil of weeds and the plant would flourish: it is unthinkable.

I am not saying their view is bad, anything but – simply that other cultures have often tried to grow people like show chrysanthemums, with pruning and staking and a paper bag over their heads, and that our passion for the undistorted bush also implies a quite definite view of humanity.

More and more I am coming to think that our absolutely central dilemma is this: now that we know how much conditioning the subconscious affects the springs of human action, what, if anything, is left besides? Koestler's rebel hero in *Arrival and Departure* was shown how every scrap of his fiery ideals could be traced back to his sinister infancy; but Koestler did not, for all that, let him conclude that his ideals had no validity. Is the psychological process merely the means by which we perfect or spoil a blueprint already set out by God or heredity? Our emotions help us to choose our theories – but does that tell us anything either way about the theories? Plato said there were Ideas towards which we dimly groped; Freud told us a lot about how we do the groping – but do the Ideas exist or don't they?

When we come to what we think is a moral or intellectual decision, is it a real decision, or was it rigged for us back in the nursery? And if it was what does 'thinking for ourselves' *mean*?

However, if there is one thing of which these letters have convinced me, it is that there is no solving this or any other problem directly for one's children. I therefore renounce any attempt to instil any intellectual concepts whatever into the poor boy; and will simply stick to things like remembering to put on the sleeveless bib when it's carrots. Everyone else, of course, will go on persuading him – schoolteachers, friends, TV, clergy, newspapers. . . . I wonder when he'll be old enough to start reading this column?

24 · *Man's Ideal Woman*

Some men want their women to be mothers and some want them to be childlike and simple; some, one suspects, really want the Principal Boy in a pantomime. But most of the stereotypes with which, through the ages, men have deluded themselves about women carry a strong streak of hopeful self-interest.

Take, for example, the one that invariably crops up at this time of year: a mainstay of the Gambols, the *I Love Lucy* show, and a good deal of Blondie: the feather-headed blonde pouring away money on glossy packages. Since day-to-day budgeting is always in the hands of women – and they usually have a vastly shrewder idea of the market value of anything (including themselves) than their menfolk – we have to seek the underlying reason for such presentation. To my mind it is really a piece of conspicuous waste (*au* Veblen). 'I can afford a useless wife,' or 'My wife throws our money away,' carrying mainly the implication that there is a good deal of throwing money around.

One could make a tidy collection of illusions great and small: the Strindbergian hag, for example, supposed to be hard and unfeminine, when she is really the she-wolf defending her young. Or there is that dotty piece of French mythology: '*Elle est une force de nature,*' they say, as they step hastily back. In the illusion of the utterly uncontrolled woman (even Simenon has a tigress gang mother in *Maigret's Special Murder*) they cherish the idea of owning a piece of the jungle: all these dull little men in hard collars want a great panther crashing through the windows of the conservatory. It falls down, of course, because they can't control her either: Jules in *Jules et Jim* only got what was coming to him when nature girl drove the car off the bridge.

One illusion which is, I suspect, at the back of a good many male minds is that embodied in the tale of Patient Griselda, who was stripped of home, income and even children without letting out a single squawk; it appears in Beatrice in *The Dutch Courtesan*, called virtuous because she never expected her lover to confine his attentions to her, and the dream figure of G.I.s who talk wistfully of Japanese women scrubbing the backs of their overlords. It is the fond hope that if only he could get a woman long-suffering enough, his own short-comings would cause no trouble at all.

Close to Griselda in some respects is the distant lady of the courtly love ideal. This female was inaccessible, because (a) virtuous and (b) married; male emotions were therefore reduced to a purity in which they need do absolutely nothing about her. They slew dragons, true – but there was no reason to suppose the lady cared about dragons either way; it was their deeds of derring-don't that more immediately concerned her.

This must be the most restful ideal ever devised (it has strong links with the sexy but unavailable Playboy Bunnies). The courtly ladies acted as a kind of externalized conscience, a holy grail in which reposed the best aspirations of their knights. As with all externalized consciences, from priests to policemen, the great attraction is that a man can go away and leave them: the ladies who held this sacred chalice for their warriors were much like the people who get stuck holding a glass of water against the ceiling with a walking-stick.

The Principal Boy illusion is found most in pre-war thrillers. The Buchan girls are brave, flat-hipped and impervious to wet shoes; in Sapper, the girl is described as 'the sort of girl who beagles when she goes beagling'. Partly this is a simple literary device: fast action has no room for twittering passengers. But it is also an expression of that great British longing of Professor Higgins's song: *Why can't a woman be more like a man?*

Trained among men in public schools, nervous and alarmed at real femininity (which, like glue, gets into everything and is hard to get off your hands) they long for a woman who scores as such only for routine purposes of plot and procreation.

And Ian Fleming's nymphomaniacs are in exactly the same position. James Bond, who uses sex as a gun symbol, expects his females to leap into bed or bush with a speed and lack of complication that is entirely masculine. In real life, women are always trying to mix something up with sex – religion or babies or hard cash; it is only men who long for sex separated out, without rings or strings.

The same longing, I suppose, has led to another recurrent figure: the tart with a heart of gold, from Moll Flanders to Maggie May. One logical conclusion of the male desire for sex and nothing else is, of course, the girl you can buy. But the snag is that if you can buy her for a fiver, someone else can win her from you for £6 7s 6d and a luncheon voucher. Hence the plaintive desire for the golden-hearted tart: the bought girl who will actually (from love) *stay* bought.

Maybe the most persistent illusion of all is the do-it-yourself model, the dream of making an ideal girl to specifications. Galatea had this trouble: so did King Cophetua's beggar maid, so did Nicole in F. Scott Fitzgerald's *Tender is the Night*, marrying the man who cured her madness. It seems a tempting notion: if the girl owes everything to man, surely he will not only be boss, he will be God?

It is a pity that the women simply cannot stand living with all that gratitude: Galatea becomes a screaming Eliza Higgins, Nicole finds a lover, the beggar maid, one suspects, hoofs off with the spoons, leaving a rude note in the throne room about kingly condescension. Men, too, can get bored with their own creations, since what they have made can hardly offer them any surprises; but the temptation to do an Identikit job of the Ideal Woman is very strong.

The problem of Galatea is really the problem of any woman, in fiction or out, who gets crammed into the golden mould of someone else's stereotype: she scrambles out, swearing, as fast as she can. And if no man gets his ideal woman, it could be simply because she does not exist; and when you think what the ideals are like, a jolly good thing too.

25 · Woman's Ideal Man

When I wrote a few weeks ago about the illusions men have about women, I fully expected some male colleague to leap forward with a companion piece on female illusions. But since no one has, I am venturing – backed up, I am happy to say, by some shrewd shafts from male readers – to tackle it myself.

Even on the everyday level, female illusion is boundless. Look at the way women think bows in the hair make them look sexy, or that it was marriage he was proposing, or that you are invisible without make-up, so that your husband is supposed to fall about when you are got up to go out, but simply not see you slopping around normally. Hans Schneider, of Marks and Spencer, speaks with peculiar bitterness of the illusion of size sixteen women that they are still size fourteen – and indeed this delusion has swept America to such an extent that all the sizes have moved down one, and they think they have abolished the size twenty-two woman altogether.

Groups of men, too, attract a special brand of misconception: you hear women talking about manufacturers as if they were a hard-eyed cabal, whose ruthless efficiency in combining to do down the consumer makes the Kremlin look like the Egg Marketing Board. And when it comes to Paris, the couturiers are thought of not as a set of dotty individuals trying hard to sell clothes, but as a massed band of torturers forcing women into sacks as if they were then going to throw them into the Bosphorus.

But it is romantic illusion, of course, that we really prefer. It is hard to track this through literature, as one could with male illusion, simply because until the nineteenth century it was mostly men doing the writing. But the nineteenth century did its best to make up for lost time.

It began with a bang: Jane Austen saying: 'It is a truth universally acknowledged, that a single man in possession of a good fortune must be in want of a wife.' And the Brontës have just about the complete catalogue. Look at Heathcliff, for example. He may not exactly beat his breast and say: 'Me Tarzan – you Cathy,' but he is clearly the first of a long line of glorious beasts. (It is our illusion of liking the jungle man that gives the Rolling Stones and the Beatles half their appeal, and takes the conviction out of our voices as we urge our menfolk to shave.)

The trouble with beasts, though, is that their presence accords so badly with the care of the beastlets they beget, not to say with civilization generally: hence the particular appeal of the half-tamed, the drawing-room animal. It is only because Emily Brontë is above such cheating that we don't get the domestic Linton and the wild Heathcliff rolled into one.

I think it is this desire for a cave-trained Neanderthal that also accounts for the cad syndrome (Elinor Glyndrome, good old East Lynnedrome) and the Arab on his steed – both are wild men with a veneer of civilization, not to be compared with the real rough stuff our heroine might have encountered, say, a bit farther south. Not that the Arab thing is ever really thought through – the female imagination stops at the point where he flings her across the crupper of his horse: it does not look forward to being dumped in the sand dunes or added to an overcrowded harem.

My favourite of this breed is the literate pirate up *Frenchman's Creek*. Real pirates, one supposes, use coarse language, rarely wash and smell piercingly of rum: this after-shave ad pirate wrote poetry and studied wild birds. It is the *noble* savage we really want – the man who, like the cabby in the old *Punch* joke, will drive like HELL – but carefully.

Sometimes, in the dream-life, women go all out for nobility alone – the *cavaliere servente*, the man who will pick up your gloves and call round with a bunch of red roses every Tuesday and Friday for five years. It is pretty far-fetched, this one, since it depends on the idea that it is the force of his passion for you that keeps him at it; whereas if he were really all that passionate he'd either crash through the bedroom door on a dark Saturday or pack it in after six months and take his roses elsewhere.

Gentleness has its place in female dream life, though – and again the Brontës have a word for it: the word is 'Professor'. Women who realize that they are, by now, too civilized to want their men simply to knock them down, wish to be mentally dominated: hence the appeal of the guru, the curate, the teacher. It has a lot of advantages. It is very high-minded; the rapture 'is in the senses but seems to be in the soul'. It overrides any other little drawbacks the man may have, such as being paunchy, Teutonic and given to saying 'Ach, so,' as does the Professor that Jo marries in *Good Wives*. And it has a comforting safety factor for the socially unsure: at the same time that you are feeling noble for appreciating the hidden beauties of the fellow you can also trust that they are too hidden to attract the scavenging attentions of your rivals.

Then there is the idea embodied in Jean Webster's phrase: 'I will marry an undertaker and be an inspiration to him in his work.' Women do have this thing about inspiring their mates, and I suppose people like Dorelia (assets included huge limbs, a tiny head and Augustus John) actually did it. I list it as an illusion because of the truly awful behaviour it provokes in those who merely *think* they are inspiring. They come into a man's studio with cups of coffee: they lay a sympathetic hand on the hangover; and the waves of their 'understanding' penetrate so successfully even through three closed doors that they can often make a man stop work altogether. No wonder the woods are full of ex-future Poets Laureate.

But the commonest source of female illusion, I suppose, is the idea that they are being good wives and girlfriends when they are actually being good mothers. The women's magazines foster this wholeheartedly. Mariolatry does nothing to dispel it (how sad that mother and maiden was never none but *she*), and it is the origin of the idea that men prefer fat women. (It is this known preference for fat women, of course, that explains why there are no film stars weighing less than eighteen stone.) But it is *mothers* who are better fatter – more shoulder to cry on, more lap to climb into.

And a reader (thanks, Mr. Wilkinson) has pointed out that the American TV serial and strip-cartoon man, a bumbling idiot unable to put up the simplest picture without falling through the third step of the ladder, is produced not by women, but for women: women who are really in search of a baby boy, to mother, protect – and despise.

The only trouble with all this is that not a word of it may be true. For the biggest illusion of all is our tendency to think that 'My husband thinks' is the same as 'Men think' and that 'I think' equals 'Women think'. So all our generalizations about ourselves may well be false.

Including, of course, that one.

26 · A Fine Time to be Alive

Now that it has more central heating and fewer mouldering gibbets, the countryside is more pleasant than it was. But it is still agreeable to get back to town after a country Christmas, simply because so many people in the country seem positively to detest the times we live in. The sixties, to them, mean nothing but pylons and noise and overcrowding, tradespeople failing to call and charwomen being wasted in factories; the country is going to the dogs, and even the dogs aren't what they were.

It is an attitude ably summed up by the headmaster of Harrow who, I am told, when he looked out of his train window at Slough, shuddered, and said: 'Not our century, is it?' I must say it is very much mine, and maybe the New Year is as good a time as any to stand up for it.

We may as well start the argument in the usual place – with those technical and scientific achievements usually dismissed in one scornful half-sentence about moon rockets and electric shoe-polishers. But I think one should spare a better word for them. Dirty nappies are dirty nappies in any age – but more people have washing machines or Paddi Pads than ever had skivvies to wash for them – and, anyway, what about the skivvies?

Modern medicine I am not inclined to pooh-pooh, having survived acute appendicitis; and I cannot help wondering whether the people who long for the peace and poetry of the eighteenth century have considered what dying in child-birth without anaesthetics must have been like. Nor is it all utilitarian, either – how many people (except friends of blind violinists) made love to music before this century?

A good many of the shots commonly aimed at the sixties seem to me simply wide of the mark. Violence, for example. Nowadays, it is true, the youths have the transport to carry their brawls into nice neighbourhoods; but you get a lot less razor-fighting in the Gorbals. Noise – but can *anything* have been noisier than iron hooves on cobbles? Again, we are supposed to have substituted telly-goggling for the home arts, but to my mind it is not the people who used to go in for part-songs and barbola work who now stare blankly at the TV, but those who used to stare blankly at the wallpaper.

Youth is supposed to be bored and aimless; yet the figures for every hobby you can name are on the increase, and any of the young that one meets seem to be full of confidence and zip. But even if all these things were true, I am still not sure it would not be outweighed by the vast increase in the freedom of choice enjoyed by the lower orders – by which I mean working people, young people and, above all, women.

You hear people asking at dinner parties what real benefits the liberation of women has, after all, brought: the poor things, they say, were a good deal more serene when they knew their role in society and stuck to it. For the minority who enjoy above all things talking and working with men the benefits are obvious: nuns, no doubt, were always allowed to work and tarts to talk, but doing both and being respectably married as well is quite an innovation.

But in arguing about this people often forget that the biggest advance is in women's legal strength *as* women – freedom to hang on to their own children, for example, to have some sort of legal share in a disbanded home; it has been a long haul from the removal of Caroline Norton's children by her unfaithful husband, to the dust-up in 1945 when they decided to let mother have the family allowances.

It is women, too, who have mainly benefited from the

let-up in family tyranny. I knew a woman, now dead, who spent her whole life as a dependent spinster because her Congregationalist father refused to let her marry her beloved Anglican. Beatrix Potter's parents were still balking at her choice of mate when she was forty, and Florence Nightingale wasted fifteen years picking up her mother's hairpins in the cause of family duty. It was she, too, who coined the phrase 'busy idleness' for the awful genteel boredom that went with the 'age of leisure'. That the servants were downtrodden we all accept, but a lady's existence must have been pretty restricted too: think of the number of things a nice woman simply did not do – including all the activities covered by that story of the Victorian bride who was sternly told on her wedding night that 'ladies do not move'.

And while we are on the subject of marriage, it is worth pointing out that for all the high proportion of failures, our *ideal* of marriage must be one of the highest the world has ever had. The notion of a complete sharing at every level; of fathers taking as much interest in the children's upbringing as mothers, of mothers really understanding a man's working life: this can hardly have been possible when the man's world and the woman's world were so separate that they overlapped only at bed and table. We talk about problems of communication; but a hundred years ago people operated in such separate grooves that they didn't *have* to communicate.

The most serious charge against the time, I suppose, is the decline in morals. But even here there may be something on the credit side. For one thing, you no longer have a situation where the respectable paterfamilias keep one prostitute in business for every two of them; and although I realize that we keep to our current proportion of one per 4000 only by the profusion of our private arrangements, I still think there is something fundamentally more honest about what Willy Stone called 'Fellers sleeping with other fellers' sisters'.

And there is another dimension to morality since socialism: nobody now supposes that you can be a good Christian slumming in ermine and pearls. The most horrifying thing about Cecil Woodham Smith's book about the Irish famine (*The Great Hunger*), it seems to me, was not the sufferings of the starving or even the callousness of the evicting landlords, but the fact that no one seemed to think the famine their responsibility. Whatever disasters happen nowadays, we do assume that somebody ought to do something; that at any rate it is our business. I don't think you can rate our morals without considering the increase in the social conscience, which is the bit this century has added to the available ideology.

In the regrettable absence of a time machine, it may seem pretty futile to ask whether these are good times to live in at all. But the point is that the things that are badly wrong with our times – the ugliness, the remaining social injustice, the sluggishness of the national tripes – are not to be put right by nostalgically looking back to a golden age that never was. Social justice is not to be had by deploring the Welfare State as a piece of modern nonsense, but by repairing the holes in its fabric. It is not the preservation of rural England, but more exciting suburban architecture which is going to make the place look better.

The Royal Dukes may be as rich as Clore, but they can no longer command a policeman to arrest me. Widows' pensions are not what they might be – but at least the poor don't receive the scraps of Blenheim Palace mixed indiscriminately like pigswill, as they did till an American put a stop to it. We may not have the serene certainty that God is on the side of the British Empire – but at least He isn't on the side of father, either. And even if we have to make up our own minds how we should behave as women, at least we don't have to behave like ladies. It may be worth living in the sixties for that alone.

27 · How Private Can You Get?

What do you expect to find behind a door marked 'PRIVATE'? The optimistic hope for the cellar or the staff bathroom; my husband says he expects to find somebody doing nothing; me, I always seem to land the broom cupboard. But whatever you expect, there is obviously a good deal of confusion about what can and cannot be legitimately defended as privacy.

Personal privacy, of the sort implied by such phrases as privy and private parts, seems simple enough. But for all that I think the taboo nature of naked flesh confuses the issue. Take (no offence meant) a bath. Sure, most of us bath without clothes; but that is not the main point: the family crashing in for aspirins is far less of an intrusion on the hour alone with book, bath salts, coffee and the tweezers than cats, who walk round the edge of the bath, stare pointedly at one's navel and even, as kittens, settle down purring on anything above sea level.

Again, with breast-feeding, one's own mother pointedly not looking as she fetches a book shatters one's privacy in a way in which six random mothers busy plugging their own infants' mouths in a hospital ward simply do not. It's the attention that causes the interference.

Indifference, even in crowds, itself makes for a sort of privacy. Billy Graham was so shocked by the behaviour of couples coupling in British parks because he failed to grasp that the reticent British count on the other British not to look: and one can create a private island in a busy news room simply by narrowing the focus of one's attention in a way you never can in a matey office for two or three.

And even the private soldier has this form of protection – in fact calling him more private than his officer is not quite as dotty as it sounds. An officer, by claiming public rank, does forfeit at least some of his right to be any sort of a man he pleases; a private has only to do certain things, not become them.

The question of how far a public man has a right to personal privacy brings up, I suppose, the question of the Press, who are always over a barrel for peering through the bung-hole. And I suppose there are cases where they do make a harmless person's life intolerable. But my shame on behalf of my profession is always a bit tempered by the patchiness of this desire to be left alone. That frightful TV series *Front Page Story* did at least hit one nail on the head when it showed a spectacular scandal in which the Press were alerted in the first instance by one of the parties concerned.

The starlet whose Press agent sends out handouts about her engagement is in a poor position for protesting if the reporters also show an interest in her divorce; no doubt it was idiotic of the voters of Stratford to put in Profumo for family virtue instead of skill in governing, but if they did they've a right to know whether their idol is cardboard or not.

Just how far this extends to the people who, while financially sustained by the public, prefer to remain faceless, is another matter; but I am not convinced that the man whose say-so (through the power of a vast insurance company, say) can change the face of my village or bank balance overnight has a cast-iron case for staying private and unknown to me.

I would even hold some sort of brief for intruding into just those institutions which hate it most: public schools, for example, may be better than secondary moderns at keeping their boys out of trouble, but I don't know how sure you can be of it when they are also so much better at keeping out of the limelight.

One can have a lot of political fun, too, with those whose claim to be only minding their own private business always sounds a bit like the people in the United Nations saying their skulduggeries are purely domestic. My favourites along these lines are Locke, who, having been at some pains to explain that a man's right to property depended on his mixing his own labour with the raw material, then innocently cited 'the turf my servant cuts' as an example; and Paul Chambers, who, from the top of the vast complex of I.C.I., sings the praises of something he calls *private* enterprise.

And not only politics but ethics are tied up in the idea: I am blowed if I see myself how a privacy defended by a long lawn, a big dog or an attitude of keeping ourselves to ourselves is consistent with any form of Christianity except the monastic – though it is obviously easier to love a neighbour you don't actually have to meet.

The trouble is that while admittedly no man is an island, anyone constantly overwhelmed by waves of other people might just as well be Atlantis anyway. But I think it is important to work out what the boundaries are, even if only for purely social purposes. No sane person can conduct his entire life under the eyes of other people. If you try, you soon get the idea that what doesn't go in public doesn't go at all. You see the corroding effects of this in bunches of teenagers who are afraid to do anything alone; or in the Truby King thirties where, having noticed that no one looks a bigger fool than someone googling at a baby, they sternly cut the googling right out. What was really needed was the realization that babies need the googling as much as they need their bottoms wiped – but that neither is necessarily an enthralling spectacle for one and all.

I read the other day the appalling suggestion that children

would grow up more balanced if they were in at the family deaths *and births* – why, even pets are allowed to be alone in the clothes cupboard (besides, can't you just imagine it: 'I want an iced lolly!' 'Hush, dear, Mummy's having a contraction'). Few things are more irritating than the couples who spoon around on the sofa while ostensibly making general conversation, and the whole bitter argument about home movies would be stilled by the simple assumption that they are an expression of family love as private and personal as old love-letters.

For the absurd thing is that if someone does in public something that they ought to do in private, it is the bystanders privacy that is infringed. By all means go ahead and pick your teeth – but not, please, where the private citizens can see you.

28 · The Grievance Cupboard

Female journalists often find themselves in the position of the girl in 'The Pajama Game', who arrived in the boss's office with the words: 'I am the grievance committee.' Oxfam may be first, surtax relief for married women about 495th, but the snag is that, making about the same amount of noise about them all, a weekly journalist can give the impression they are all equally important.

As a way of putting off the more strenuous sort of spring cleaning I am this week clearing out the grievance cupboard, in the usual pious hope of being able to send most of it to the jumble sale.

The first things to fall out of the cupboard are, of course, the hats – in this case, Green Hats. A girl I was at school with once woke up shouting 'Green Hats for all!' and this is a fair description of those rows which are strictly luxuries – attempts to get theatres open on Sunday or have the Swingle Singers jailed for the murder of good music. You get the same pleasure from these as from watching two thoroughly nasty scholars tearing each other apart in the *New Statesman*: you don't have to worry about the outcome. These, I suppose, could certainly go.

At the other end of the scale there are the indispensable ones: the ones you cannot abandon however long they have been there, however weary you are of them: like bandages and brandy, they are a matter of life and death. These are the fights for more education, less world hunger; for social justice and religious freedom: they stay, and the problem is to make their threadbare appearance once more compelling.

But there is a vast amount in between. There are the ones which are no doubt of good quality but not, if you see what I mean, quite *me*. When in doubt, throw it out; everyone has to let themselves off *some* of the world's worries, and there are several I can do without.

Animal causes, for a start: the factory farming ones *are* serious, I admit, though I am prepared to leave them to others; but when it comes to the disappearance of the lesser tit-throated whitebait or the need to preserve noble, nearly extinct beasts (such as lions and Great Christian Gentlemen), my withers are so unwrung as to be positively drip-dry. And the Cause of Sport – if those who clamour about it mean more open spaces for slum kids, they rarely make it clear; otherwise, surely, if people want to do it or watch it, it has some point, and if not, how can it need aid? Away with it.

The trickiest category of causes, though, consists of those that do matter madly in the short run, but pale a bit when you look at them through the wrong end of a global telescope. I have to admit that at a pinch we could do without just about all the food grievances (except perhaps the ones about toxic effects); no one is more ready than I am to spring up and denounce the maker of fake-smoked hake or sneer at the butchers who can't present a cheap joint properly. But one cannot honestly say the world would be that much the worse if nobody ever ate anything again that *didn't* taste of Monosodium glutamate, provided everyone got fed.

The whole consumer movement, too, really deals in Grade B grievances, I am afraid. It is essentially a piece of enlightened self-interest, and though there are dedicated and selfless people working for it, a great crusade for fabrics you can't shrink is not in the same league as a fight for judges you can't bribe.

For all that, it is this sort of grievance which affects most obviously the lives of all those not actually on the bread line or the brink of suicide; and it is harder to sort out the priorities in these Quality-of-the-National-Life causes than any others. I think there is a fundamental division between those who think it a scandal that it was so hard to raise the money to save the Leonardo cartoon and those who would rather spend the money on, say, bigger pensions or a better bus service.

I am not even sure you cannot divide people politically by whether they feel more strongly about slum clearance or beautiful architecture, first-rate opera or pop shops for all, a world safe for Dior to live in or one where you can actually get the dress in your size. And I suspect that one of the reasons that artists, when they are Left at all, are very Left indeed, is because they have to resist such a force pulling them in the opposite direction: in the direction of a leisured class with time to spend on the arts.

But whether this is so or not, there are those who think that things like the National Theatre and the design of teacups are major causes, not minor; they argue that the drabness of the streets of Lancashire do harm to our very soul; and they can reach the extremes of human passion as they report that they saw Esau sitting on an eyesore. To them, aesthetic grievances are Grade A, the stuff of civilization.

I can't agree with them. I agree with E. M. Forster, who realized how little taste had to do with happiness: in *The Longest Journey* the scholar gets on well with his grocer father, partly *because* neither of them has any taste to disagree about. Walls running with damp, or children who never come down from high flats to play, are things which really affect people; the design of the building does not. To me, aesthetics are a Class B grievance, however little I want to dispense with them altogether.

I once asked a well-known philanthropist which had been his favourite causes; and, flushed with wine, he had some difficulty in remembering; finally he said he used to carry a tremendous torch for box-pleated skirts for the A.T.S. I

29 · Incompleat Housewife

It had to happen, I suppose. After the anti-intellectual, the anti-believer, and, above all, that scruffy, incapable young man the anti-hero, we now have the anti-housewife. A series of booklets out last week makes me realize that neither Peg Bracken with her *Hate to Cook* and *Hate to Housekeep* books, nor I with my shambling band of sluts, is as original as we might have hoped. We are part of a trend.

The booklets – the *Awful Dressmaker's, Handyman's, Cook's Books** – are like the ones sent back with your snaps from photographers, saying, 'The mistakes you have made are described on page . . .' (in my case always left blank, they are described on *all* pages). The booklets are subtitled: 'How do you put it right if you've messed it up?' Any dressmaker will recognize 'Sleeves in Wrong Armholes' or 'Lumps in the Hem'; obviously cooks who find themselves with 'Stewed Apples Falling to Pieces' or 'Stuffing Falling out of a Roast Joint' are as common as colds; and the Awful Handyman not only hits the wood instead of the nail and lets the paintbrush set solid, but also paints and varnishes furniture and then wishes she hadn't. I say 'she', for if we are being as realistic as all that, we need hardly pretend that men do all the odd jobs round the house. Sure they do – if you have two or three years to spare.

The practical advice is not so very different from that contained in more optimistic manuals; for it is distressing how often the longest way round *is* the shortest way home. The day I went to a ball in a dress for which, at ten that morning,

* *The 'Awful Books'*, Wolfe Publishing, 3s 6d.

I had not even bought the material, I remember that I followed the directions to the letter – at least to the point where they said 'Hem it' and I reached for the sticky tape.

What is different in these books is the settled melancholy of their expectations: it is like the difference between the ghastly vigour of those 'Lift up Your Hips' early-morning P.T. programmes and the one on American TV which begins with a groaning man groping for an aspirin. What interests me is why there should be such an appeal in an approach which presupposes a disgusted and reluctant homemaker rather than one who is clean, eager and competent.

The first explanation, I think, is a simple reaction against the perfectionism of women's mags. and women's ads. They get despairing in the suburbs, I am told, at the discrepancy between this plastic heaven, where hair is always clean and shining, children freckled and endearing and the kitchens new and spotless, and real life in which the kids kick the furniture and you never get time even to comb your hair, let alone dream-shampoo it.

By remorselessly cheering women up, the mags. and ads. in fact depress them extremely; though so long as women keep desperately hoping that one more twee gadget or a new shoe polish will save the day, the advertisers aren't bothered. Still, it does leave the field free for anyone who comes round reassuring them that we have all missed the same boat together.

Then there is the puzzled anger we all feel at the time-saving devices which don't, in practice, seem to leave us with any time saved. When I hear people denouncing appliances in general, I always wonder what I would do without, for example, the dryer that stops the wet clothes dripping dankly into the cooking, or the basket on wheels that halves my shopping trips, and, *of course*, a washing machine is an improvement on the washboard and it is sentimental to pretend it isn't.

But what cancels out the effectiveness of the labour-saving age is, first, that there is no really satisfactory mechanism yet for ironing, washing up or tidying (wait till I patent my magnetic clothes-scoop); secondly, that half of us haven't got even the machines that do exist, though we are still needled by the dream-world of their advertisements: and, lastly, the fact that standards, with a Parkinsonianism of their own, seem always to keep one jump ahead of the devices designed to maintain them. (I think with horror of the American house-wives who use up the time saved by their fully automatic washing machines by washing the sheets twice a week.)

The other force behind the anti-housewife, I think, may be the third wave in the tide of emancipation – by which I mean votes, choices, contraceptives, short skirts and such-like. To begin with, the pioneers deliberately rejected the domestic arts, played down the question of their appearance and as-serted themselves in all the traditionally *un*feminine fields just to prove they could. They sometimes looked pretty grotesque doing it: front-line soldiers often do.

Then came a second, more relaxed, attitude. The battle being more or less won – women felt – there was no reason why they should not be equally good in the home and out of it, or why one should wear hair like a bird's nest to demon-strate the egghead within. Graduates started cooking as well as home-bodies (though they still make, according to one researcher, 'absolutely lousy housemaids'); bright girls were prepared to take on all comers and wash nappies or write reports as occasion offered.

I think we may now be coming to the realization that perhaps all this is just *too much*, and that the ideal of the female polymath can be just as artificial as the straight either/or postures of the Pankhursts. The women who are now owning up to being bad at macaroons and unable to iron tab collars have perhaps been daunted by the ideal they have to live up

30 · Holing out in One

Advice on the right remark to get you out of a social hole is not hard to come by. But the trouble with most of it is that no one has actually tried it out in test conditions: like my plan for foiling sales girls by pretending to be stone deaf, it takes too much nerve to be useful. For this reason I am starting a notebook full of things people have actually said; it should be complete enough to cover every social situation by about the time I am ninety, and can't speak anyway for fear my teeth will fall out.

I do not mean to collect those savage rejoinders we all enjoy rolling around our minds: like poor John Wilkes, to whom a man said: 'Oh, Wilkes! Thought you were dead – hanged or died on the pox.' Wilkes replied: 'That would depend, Sir, on whether I embraced your principles or your mistress.' And I shall reluctantly have to leave out my favourite bits of lifemanship – even the one that was done to me by a rival fashion editor. She praised my dress; I, to turn the compliment aside, as one does, said I liked it, too, but it was very cheap and creased dreadfully. She said: 'Oh, my dear, grey flannel *always* does that – I have one by Hardy Amies, and it does just the same.'

No: these are fine, but they aren't any use. What one wants is a sort of Cliffhanger's Manual, the handbook of the well-caught brick.

The first phrase that made me want to start such a collection came from John Chandos, taking out Fenella Fielding in one of her more startling dresses. The waiter was slow bringing the bill, but it would clearly have been churlish to suggest that he was in a hurry to end the evening. Chandos said: 'I did ask for my bill ten minutes ago but I don't suppose you took me seriously.' To this I rapidly added Cyril Ray's dinner gimmick, of great use to anyone with a reputation as a gourmet. If he says nothing his hostess is desolated; if he praises it, she'll presumably label the noxious mess 'the dish that Cyril liked', which wouldn't do at all. What he does – it took me years to spot it – is to fall about with rapture *as the dish comes to table*. 'My favourite food! Goodness, this looks delicious!' And so charmed are you with this that you hardly notice he never says a word once the stuff is actually in his mouth. As a way of implying a compliment you haven't in fact made, it is rivalled only by that classic way of thanking a thoroughly dreary speaker: 'I am sure you can tell from the volume of the applause how much we appreciated. . . .'

Two of the commonest problems are what to say when they offer a drink and you don't know if it's Scotch or coffee, and when they say, 'What are you doing on Friday?' and you don't know if it's babysitting or a First Night. The first can usually be turned off with a simple, 'What do you suggest?' and to the second a friend of mine came up with the perfect answer: 'I'm taking a sick car to Thames Ditton.' If he wanted to accept, it was amazing how fast he found he could get back. Maybe it cannot always be a sick car, but anything indefinite, like delivering a chest of drawers or visiting an aunt in jail, would do equally well.

Business has its own problems. One executive I know says that if he is asked out to dinner and doesn't know whether his wife is included, he always rings up a day or two later saying, 'I'm dreadfully sorry – *what* time do you expect us?' Presumably he could, though he doesn't, then make an excuse for his wife if the pause following this remark was unduly long. And one man has the perfect phrase for being taken out to lunch by a woman, and guarding against her turning all feminine when the bill arrives. He says: 'Does it embarrass you, taking men out to lunch?' The reverse problem can usually be solved by handing over a request or a wine list to the man, with a pretty 'Could you choose it for us?' Or: 'Could *you* ask him?' and it also helps to reverse the usual rule about not mentioning that it is on the firm: it is less embarrassing for a man to accept lunch, apparently, from Sir Hugh Greene or Cecil King than from the frail flower with the bulging pocket book.

One of the commonest driers-up of things to say is the sight of someone else's absolutely hideous six-week-old baby; and there is only one universal answer: 'He looks so like you!' For some reason the uglier the baby the more the parents are pleased by this; whereas if you tell the truth and say: 'He looks like Sid James' they are huffed to a degree. Truth, in fact, is often little help socially; in the situation where you drop something that has plainly *got* to be eaten anyway, you can only emulate the woman whose maid staggered in with the Christmas turkey and shot it on to the floor. She said: 'Take it out, Mary, and bring in the other one.'

Famous people, apparently, have their own troubles; and how they cope tells you a lot about them. If someone says 'And of course you've heard of Miss Blank', and you haven't, a starlet will pout all evening; but a *grande dame* will say 'Of course she hasn't – why should she have?' – which gives you time to pull yourself together and say 'But yes, I asked for your autograph in 1952'. She'll never anyway admit she didn't sign any autographs that year.

And one famous author, when someone looms up saying: 'I've heard *so* much about you!' says: 'Lies! All lies! And anyway she started it!' Which just goes to show that even clichés have their uses: it's a good deal easier to say: 'No, thanks, I just put one out, ha, ha,' when offered another drink, than to go into the question of whether you hate the liquid deconcern, are on a diet, or know you've had more than enough already.

There is no known answer, alas, to the worst social problem of all: how to introduce someone whose name you have forgotten; and desperate expedients like 'You two know each other, of course' or 'Julius Caesar meet Madame Chiang Kai-shek' can do little to gloss over the wound you are inflicting. Until we all hold our hands out firmly saying: 'I'm Snodgrass, pleased to meet you' as the Americans do, this one is insoluble.

At least, I would have thought so; but maybe no social pitfall is absolutely bottomless. Who would have thought, for instance, that there was any way out of *this* situation? A shy, gauche young man found himself week-ending at a very stately home indeed, and just about steered his way through the maze of valets and footmen during the evening. When he went to bed he found himself confronted with two identical buttons: he pressed one, and instead of the light going out the butler came in. But with a genius born of terror, he lay back on the pillows and said languidly, 'Just put the light out, would you?' The butler ate out of his hand from then on.

31 · Fecund to a Fault

Every time one reads of a mother leaving her baby with a minder who keeps three babies in their prams in a dark shed: or a film-world mother who comes into the nursery only to have rows with an ever-changing stream of nannies, one always asks: 'Why on earth did they ever have children at all?' The answer usually is that it simply didn't occur to them not to; and the fact that it still doesn't, in an overcrowded island liberally sprinkled with contraceptives, seems odd enough to stand investigation.

It is not just socially O.K. to have children; it is socially suspect not to. Any childless couple knows the thinly veiled sympathy with which the fecund favour them; any woman's magazine has at least one story about a down-trodden Mum whose drab life is suddenly illuminated by scorn for a sterile sister. You get Barbara Cartland telling young things not to 'play at marriage' by putting off parenthood, and David Frost talking disparagingly of the couple who have had a bubble car instead of a baby; and even in serious circles there are sour references from the pulpit about the homes where you see a telly instead of a toddler.

Over and over again people imply the 'selfishness' of the childless couple – a wry commentary on where they think self-interest really lies. But what *is* selfish about not having children, this year, next year, sometime, never? Selfishness, after all, is not a word used about something that just pleases the self (like scratching the ear or painting the ceiling purple), only about something that does it at someone else's expense (like painting your husband purple to match the ceiling).

Just *who* is supposed to be worse off if a couple that doesn't want children doesn't have them? Not society – there are too few good women workers and a bulge of babies too big for the facilities as it is. Certainly not the child – it is hardly going to profit from being born, for example, before its parents have a reasonable place to live, or from being thought of as the full stop to a man's freedom to manœuvre professionally. Yet the myth persists.

Part of it comes, of course, simply from happy mothers assuming that nobody else can be happy in any other way – and a little, at least, from rather less well-intentioned women who know that everyone gives up something for their children and don't see why anyone else should get life on what they think of as easy terms. But there is something deeper: a fear, at least among the people who control the propaganda, that unless you build up the image of Mum into a cross between the Statue of Liberty and the Virgin Mary, women will all rush off and try to become Lord Chancellor instead.

I don't myself regard this as a very grave risk: a majority of women will always want children more than anything else in the world. But I do think that in trying to plug motherhood we have laid far too much emphasis on maternal feelings and far too little on the actual child. This imbalance crops up in all sorts of ways: in discussions on birth control and even abortion which seem to regard these as a kind of good-conduct prize for mothers of six, and miss the fact that the worse the woman, the better the case for children not being born to her. It appears in the most popular picture of motherhood, the dreamy, slightly out-of-focus woman with a bundle of toothless love in her arms, which is what women think about when they get pregnant – not the fifteen-year commitment of care and concern. One wonders how many mothers wake up after four or five months surprised to discover that the soupy mysteries are over and the baby is still among those present.

It seems to me that the last way to get good mothers is to suggest that there is any particular virtue in just becoming a mother – the virtue is entirely in how you behave to your child thereafter. Awarding a Medal of Soviet Motherhood can only ensure a quantity of babies – it does nothing for the quality. Instead of urging women to be mothers, we should try to make jolly sure they aren't mothers unless they are dead keen on – I was going to say the idea, but being keen on the *idea* is easy; dead keen on children would be more to the point. You don't, after all, get good pilots by urging the entire ground crew to take to the air – but then planes are considered too valuable to risk.

I have been trying this theory out on bunches of social workers and professional councillors; and one of them made the point that although the propaganda is all for motherhood, the actual practice isn't – there are no fatherless families allowances, too few nursery schools, not enough home helps. We agreed it ought to be exactly the other way round – parenthood optional, but good care compulsory and easy. If we could once make motherhood genuinely optional – which it isn't, of course, if women feel odd and out of it if they don't produce – we could crack down a lot harder on anyone who did choose to have children: make it impossible, for example, for a woman with pre-schoolchildren to work without satisfying the local authority about child care arrangements.

And once we had contraception and so forth really as available as we all act as if it were, I fear the unmarried mothers would get it in the neck once more: not, as before, because the baby means they've been to bed, which is their own affair, but for having let a baby happen in adverse circumstances, which isn't.

No doubt it is a pipe dream to think of a situation where

it was conception that took forethought, not contraception: where you had to stick on the Pill for twenty-one days to *have* a child. But I would like to see a state where a couple would consider whether they should have a baby as cautiously as an adoption society; where the people who advise the young would give the same answer to anyone wondering whether to have a baby as they say now to anyone wondering about love, sex, or marriage: 'If there's any doubt at all in your mind, the answer's "No".' I would like to see it considered more immoral to have a baby 'to save a marriage' than to go for a divorce; and even if a few more marriages came unstuck, I am convinced the sum of human damage would be less. Grown-ups, after all, can take care of themselves.

32 · Househoping

The pleasures of buying a house are clouded by worries about the mortgage, the move, and whether the vendor is in fact selling the house you are buying. But the joy of ceasing to househunt is without flaw. Househunting in London is hell.

'All London to choose from!' you think at the start, and get out a map. However, you sensibly decide not to put Central London between the baby and its grandmothers, which eliminates half of it. You sketch in the six-mile taxi limit, if you are journalists. You rule out all areas not within striking distance of an open space and your daily woman's bus route. You then cross out the areas you think are too snob, and your husband crosses out the ones that remind him of his challenging three-part exposé of slums in the sixties; and what you are left with is about six streets.

Of these, the first is a row of modern houses, all specially certified by the R.S.P.C.A. as being unsuitable for cat-swinging; these are called family houses because you can hear the baby cry, or indeed breathe, anywhere in the house. If they have wood-framed windows they are described as Georgian, a phrase used by house agents for a house which was built by a man who was, or who knew a man who was, called George.

The next are a set of ratty old rooming houses, round which you are shown either by a prim woman in curlers (this kind smells of cheap lino and has yellowing notices beginning 'Don't . . .'), or by an Irishman in baggy trousers who has always forgotten the key to the room in which the body, the dry rot or (he says) a friend on night shift is sleeping. In both cases the plumbing has been preserved as an Historical Monument (second class). The house agents, with missionary zeal, describe these as 'Home and Income: would convert' – just as they talk piously of an Improving Mews.

After a few of these you turn eagerly to something smaller and more feasible: a mews, say, or a coach house or a pram shed. Someone has usually spent a fortune on them, which they intend to recover: there are pink bidets and Wastemasters and a lot of black mirror-glass. They sometimes have spaces at the back described variously as 'garden' (small garden), 'small garden' (yard) or 'patio' (a sort of running-board along the back of the house with one dank plant in a pot). These you learn to avoid by skipping any advertisement which includes the word bijou, dwarf, cottage or charming.

All these categories are fiendishly expensive and the remaining houses are either Hampstead borders (which extends to the Markyate exit of M1), Holland Park (anything east of Slough), very short leaseholds, scheduled for redevelopment or actually *in* a railway yard. You look at enough of them to realize that what London has most of, and what you will end up in, is simply a Victorian house in a row. It then becomes a matter of finding one that isn't either so narrow you have to go into the hall sideways or so well endowed with connective tissue that it would cost as much to heat as the Albert Hall. (We never looked at the Albert Hall. I wonder. . . .)

You learn quite a bit about house agents in the course of all this. You sicken almost at once of the house ad designed to be read as literature, and so little do you wish to know the number of lovers the owner has had (compared to the number of bedrooms she has had them in, which is omitted) that you are puzzled why anyone should print them, until one day the gaff is blown by an agent boasting in an ad that he got £2,000 *more* for a house than a local man. You realize that such ads are not aimed at you at all, but at the people with houses to sell.

You realize that if it hadn't been for all the fat years the agents who send you details of houses that are the wrong size, in the wrong part of London and double what you can possibly pay would hardly stay in business; and you realize that only by ringing round the agents every three weeks to remind them of your existence can you get them to keep you in mind at all. It dawns on you that it is only by getting deeply into the consciousness of one or two agents that you have a hope. We could have bet which agent would find us a house long before he actually did because he was the only one who was really trying intelligently.

All the time you are battering away at the agents on the one hand, you are being maddened by your friends on the other. By the people who bought a house in Keats Grove ten years ago, when it was cheap, or who got one for a song because of a sitting tenant, who then became a baby-sitting tenant or left for Madagascar; by relations in the Midlands who move blithely into a brand-new house with underfloor heating for rather less than you pay as a deposit on an un-reconstructed London dump; and by the couples you know are earning, if anything, less than you are, who nevertheless waltz into a Regency mansion with three baths, confessing shyly that Daddy had to sell some shares. Indeed, the way things are going, those with Daddies and shares will soon be the only ones living within the sound of Bow Bells at all.

Most trying of all are those who urge on you, *ad nauseam*, their own particular compromise; while politeness prevents your saying that every single house in their neighbourhood is completely hideous, and if it really takes them only twenty-three minutes to get to work on weekdays, why does it take an hour and a half to drive there on Sunday?

'It's tricky, buying a house,' Anthony Sampson once said. 'You have to decide what sort of person you are.' And it's true that you uncover layers of snobbery you never knew you had – at least if you define snobbery as anything which runs against the trend of the actual facts. You realize that your desire not to live anywhere where you might have to send your children to school with C. P. Snow's is nearly as snobbish as the worries of others about their kids 'picking up an accent'; that your concern for living in a good neighbourhood is just as pernickety as Mrs Exeter's, although she means 'near Harrods' when you mean 'near a fish-and-chip shop'.

But at the same time you realize that with houses, as with marrying people, feelings are as important as facts. You can look on the bright side of a house you've fallen for, however north it faces, whereas you can positively invent snags for a place you feel you ought to like and don't. If your husband thinks the little ones would fall into the picturesque canal, the point is not whether they would or wouldn't, but that he would worry; if the factory chimney seems to dominate you, it's no good pointing out that it doesn't actually keep off much light.

Of course the absurd thing about it all is that one should be looking for a house, in a capital city, at all. New Yorkers don't; Parisians don't; and heaven knows we, who have never even had a lavatory to ourselves, let alone a house, are flat-dwellers by nature.

But while there are houses to be had, while a proper family flat is at least as hard to come by as a house, one goes through all this, knowing guiltily that one is really darn lucky to be able to go through it at all. Roll on the day when the first four floors of all new blocks are family flats, with enclosed communal gardens, laundries in the basement, and singles and couples in smaller flats above; when you don't have to choose a good area to get a good school and the whole thing is operated by sane local authorities anyway.

But even when that millennium arrives, they'll have to pull our house down around our ears to get us to go through any of this again.

33 · Fashion From Without

There is a celebrated saga which begins:

Sire, four virgins wait without.
Without what?
Without food and clothing.
Give them food and bring them in.

How it goes on I don't know, as it is apparently unsuitable for mixed company, but having been without fashion in every sense of the word for some time now, I am interested in how very different the fashion scene looks from the other side.

I used to have high hopes, when I was fashion editor. As I broke my heels slogging up those dress manufacturers' stairs, as I arrived gloveless in the hot salons full of cool ladies, and got ink on my face answering letters beginning: 'I have a red skirt and a blue dress and a green suit: would a pink coat be more elegant with them or a yellow one?' I used to think that once I stopped concerning myself with the clothes of the women of England, I might finally emerge with enough time and know-how to get somewhere with my own. But it isn't that easy.

Certain things stuck, of course – such as the value of sending gloves to Pullar's by post for cleaning, or the importance of knowing your stocking length if they are not forever to be unaccountably above the knickers or below the knee. I seem to have acquired a taste for better fabrics than I can afford, and a more or less permanent imperviousness to salesgirls, after three years of being told, 'It's the latest from Paris,' when I knew darned well it wasn't.

But a lot of what I learnt must have been out of date within six months. I don't mean that fashion changes with such speed, but that shops, departments, brand names are suddenly different. In the fashion world all these movements are heralded by such a wealth of unkind chatter about why the buyer was sacked or whose marital crack-up resulted in all those neurotic buttons that you hardly notice the actual effect of the changes themselves. But when you don't know the inside story (all six versions of it) you notice only that a favourite shop has become unaccountably dull or that the three nicest dresses you've seen in years all have the same hitherto unknown label. Clearly, a settled policy of 'I always buy my suspenders at Sarringes' gets you nowhere in so rapidly changing a world.

Just to complicate matters, the clothes one needs outside the fashion world are also quite different. In it, what one really should have had was outfits smart enough to go on to a cocktail party when the others (the rats) had had time to go home and change. As a housewife, one at least has the advantage of always starting from home, so there need be no confusion between good clothes for going out, frightful clothes for staying in, and pram-pushing clothes – which are clothes that are meant to look as if you wear them all the time, but differ in that they have been bought within living memory and are not entirely covered in carrot.

And one's shopping patterns change, too. If one works around the West End, one is constantly exposed to temptation, so that it's often easier to buy new clothes than to look after the ones you've got; and there is the added hazard of ordering things from dress shows, so that you get something that looked marvellous on a willowy model, but simply pollarded on you. But at least you can be constantly in the shops without difficulty, and you scarcely notice the time it takes to track down the things to go with things.

When it takes a special battle plan to stage a spring offensive on the shops at all, you realize you have to allow about twice as long for matching things up as for buying the original garment. Sure you want to look like a tone poem, but it's like the poem A. E. Housman wrote, of which the first ten lines took him a morning and the other two took him three months. Even something simple and available like navy-blue can be a headache, till you feel that the right Swiss navy exists in the shops no more than it does on the high seas.

I find I am now pathetically eager to get matching co-ordinates, shoes sold with a handbag of the same leather, a dress and coat to match – anything to avoid going around like the Prince's messenger in Cinderella, waving a slipper at everyone in town. Small wonder that plenty of women think, with Henry Ford, that the thing is to have any colour you like as long as it's black.

But the really heartening thing about being out of fashion is that it becomes so much easier to tell what the fashion is. Partly, of course, because you can simply ring up someone who is in it and say, 'Georgina, what are skirts?' and she, having spent five weary months finding out, says 'Shorter.' But also because you can wait so much longer to decide. When you see, as we used to see, a whole lot of clothes in May, it was extremely hard to guess which, after another Paris, would catch on in the autumn; and the manufacturers themselves didn't know half the time.

We used to spend long, painful hours wondering if we'd got it right; wondering, too, if anyone ever took the slightest notice when we said that collars were pointed and shoes weren't. Now that I am on the receiving end of all this, I see we needn't have worried. Every time you cast a casual eye over a magazine, glance at the shops from the top of a bus or vaguely notice that your friends seem to be wearing new stockings, what you are really doing is building up, piece by unconscious piece, an idea of a general look, an image in your mind that will enable you to say 'That looks right'; and it doesn't matter that you don't know exactly why.

And what heaven it is *not* having to worry about why; simply saying, 'I like it'; *not* bothering about whether it will sweep the country; merely asking if they have it in my size and *not* arguing about whether it comes in enough sizes for the readers. And it is splendidly restful to wear an old favourite without being raked by those all-knowing dress-trade eyes that can put a date, brand label and price tag on everything you have on: 'You look so modern in your sixteen-shilling hat,' Otto Lucas once said to me. 'Twenty-nine and elevenpence, please!' I said, affronted. 'No,' he said, 'I mean *to make*.'

But there is no real escape from the sartorial problem – not even in the academic cloisters. I had to wear a gown at a meeting a month or two ago. First I had to brave a military department, all epaulettes and regimental badges, to collect it; then my secretary had told them I was four inches shorter than I am and they had sat up all night making a Courrèges shorty of it; and when I finally wore it at the meeting, one woman said: 'Hm! Only a B.A. – pity,' and another said: 'I do hope you don't mind my mentioning it, but you don't put your arms through *there*, but through *there*.' You not only can't win – you can't even not play.

34 · Odd Facts of Life

I once read about a man who said the only thing he could remember his mother teaching him was that you got ingrowing toenails if you cut them rounded instead of across. What surprises me is that, if he knew it was his mother who told him, the information made such an impression: for it often seems that the facts we best remember come from the most forgotten and unlikely sources.

You get facts from films: hundreds of people must have driven over level-crossings at fifty miles an hour since the lorry drivers in *The Wages of Fear* reckoned that speed was less likely to blow up their nitro-glycerine than slowing down. And I know an exasperated designer of helicopters who reckons that a whole generation of aeronautical engineers has been bedevilled by the idea of metal fatigue contained in Nevil Shute's *No Highway*.

You get them from advertisements: if you read that 'Only Sick-o-Mat has enough enzymes for your cat' you soon forget the cat and the cat-food, but you are still left with the impression that cats need enzymes – or at any rate that enzymes exist. You even get facts from tea-towels now that they are all covered with cheeses and herbs and geography – it is only a matter of time before someone puts in *Who's Who* 'educated at home from tea-towels' (Sir John Newsom would say it was the perfect education for girls, I suppose).

Look at the amount of information one mops up in the course of a detective story – at the end of Dorothy Sayers's *The Nine Tailors* you may not know much about men and death, but you know a fantastic amount about bells. And think of all the botany you get from a pastoral poet – all the nature study I know comes out of A. E. Housman, and I find myself muttering 'the plum broke forth in green, the pear stood high and snowed', to distinguish between one that has the blossoms before the leaves and the other that is the tallest tree blooming.

One could almost write a history of the indirect effects of literature; what effect had *Look Back in Anger* on the incidence of ironing on Sundays among the intellectual classes? Did the sale of corn-cobs in Memphis, Tennessee, go up or down after Temple Drake was raped with one in *Sanctuary*? 'Did any word of mine send out Certain men the English shot?' wondered W. B. Yeats. Maybe so, maybe not; but I bet a whole lot of people know that bees build in starlings' nests who didn't until he wrote poems about it.

You might think people would be sceptical of such haphazard sources of information – and I daresay they would be, if only they remembered what they were. But a lot of our most fervent beliefs apparently come from nowhere. Where did I read that if you chop the legs off flies for a hundred generations the flies get fed up and stop growing legs? It's apparently quite untrue, but I've believed it for years – and now I believe the equally anonymous source that told me it ain't so.

And I found myself explaining the other day that the William Tell legend had, in fact, started in ancient Egypt – till someone let out a yell and reminded me I'd got the idea from an Ed Fisher cartoon, which showed some archaeologists unearthing a mural of a man shooting an apple off someone's head; the caption ran, 'The Swiss aren't going to like this.' Yet I had vaguely remembered it as a fact – and I daresay at least one person will vaguely remember it as a fact *from this explanation*.

You can see the self-perpetuating nature of unchecked

141

notions at their best in the beauty business. There the idea that some particular trick creates a particular effect is repeated from one woman to another until it suddenly goes out of date and is seen to be nonsense – like the blob of rouge on showgirls' ears (I got *that* from Edna Ferber). My most hilarious experience of such blind faith was a school play I once saw where the teacher who did the make-up thought that eyeshadow should be *red*; of course the wretched heroine got more of it than anyone else, and so looked even more like a newly-hatched bird with a hangover than the rest of them.

Sex, too, is marvellous territory for extraordinary dogmas. There was a girl at school who used to assert confidently that 'a man can't write a poem for three months after . . . you know'. And I heard recently of a couple in the thirties whose attempts to determine the sex of their child were based on two alternative posibilities: first, that the sex of the child was the sex of the more ardent partner; and second, that the ovaries send down male and female eggs month and month about. Where they can have *got* all this, I don't know – they probably hardly knew themselves.

It is this, really, that makes it so hard to root out mistakes: the fact that, like bindweed, you never know where they start. They say that in the Army the way to disguise the fact that you've let half a dozen water-carts slide over a cliff into the sea is to send authority one memo lamenting the loss of six water-bottles, and another, ten days later, saying, 'In previous memo for "bottles" read "carts" ' – of which naturally no one takes the slightest notice. The same is apt to be true of any correction, any reassessment, any denial: it never catches up with the origins of the mistake.

And some are gone past recall. Alan Brien has recently been collecting up in the *Spectator* a whole lot of stories constantly told as 'it happened to a friend of mine' – like the perennial about the dog that ate the family fish, and was found dead;

and only after the family had been stomach-pumped to the last aunt the dog turned out to have been run over. He calls it folk-lore, and it is; but an awful lot of folk-lore goes around looking like straight information: Tomas the Rimer nowadays is got up like a scientist, and says 'Statistics show. . . .'

This is each person's revealed religion: the things they know, but know not how they know. Facts whose origin has vanished become indisputable. I know a man – indeed, I am married to him – who feels affronted if you suggest that hibernating bears do not stamp about on blueberries to cake their paws with a handy snack for the winter. If any scientist had actually crawled up to the bears' paws to suck them and see, and written a paper about it, this man would be the first to be sceptical. How many bears had he interviewed anyway? And how did he know the bear planned to eat them, and hadn't just forgotten to wipe its feet? But because this man has known this all his life, he *knows* it is true. It is not open to argument. It is a fact. And I daresay if the bears cut their toenails on the round, they will ingrow among the blueberries at that.

35 · *Living With Sex*

(One of four commentaries on Wayland Young's book *Eros Denied*.)

If one has to take sides at once, I am unhesitatingly *for* the sexual revolution: no amount of chaos could be worse than the cruelties and restraint, humbug and suffering that went with the idea that sex was sinful.

But the subject is not as simple as that. And one thing that Wayland Young and the more joyous and confident revolutionaries leave out is that sex is *dangerous* (D. H. Lawrence had no illusions about this). It is a natural force, like fire; and like fire it can weld and warm or it can destroy. The problem of all sexual morality, I take it, is to reduce the danger without reducing the power; in conventional morality you steer clear of sex except under asbestos conditions; with the new permissiveness you attempt a sort of scorched earth policy, the 'Why should anybody mind?' approach. It may be more attractive than the alternative, but it has its snags.

Fortunately it is possible for people at the Puritan end of the scale to take a look at what is happening at the other: for the two are so far apart that if you suggest in Chelsea that a man should try *not* to sleep with other girls while his wife is away, you don't get a much better reception than poor Dr Peter Henderson, medical officer to the Ministry of Health, did, when he suggested (albeit among consenting adults) that engaged couples were not actually damned if they slept together. And in the places where the freedom is nearly complete – journalism, say, or the stage – there is a sort of 'sleeping up with the Jones' ethos that puts the faithful and the virgin, if any, badly on the defensive; it is the man who *doesn't* go off

144

to the red light district on a Press trip who is apt to feel odd man out, not the other way round. In the age of freedom it is 'that rarest of sexual perversions, chastity', that is least readily allowed.

However, at the present rate of going, chastity will have died out altogether in another fifty years, and the handout which good and responsible people are currently offering the young is, to my mind, doing nothing to help. The old Christian prohibitions made sense in two ways: the doctrine of original sin taught that *all* sex was sinful unless sanctified, and the fear of fatherless children gave the theological doctrine a practical sanction. But nowadays the doctrine is one which only a fraction of people even understand, let alone believe; contraception has diminished the force of the pregnancy deterrent; andthe rule seems simply a dry and pointless 'no'.

Teachers and parents offer a flat rule, and it doesn't come across as an ideal: *Towards a Quaker View of Sex*, predictably rejected by the sect's stuffier members, is one of the few things written on the subject which seems to be *as* idealistic as the feelings of a couple in love.

Perhaps the young *are* told that integrity consists of mind, body and spirit working in the same direction; that sex that involves the whole personality is better than sex from the waist down; but the message comes across weak and faint. One gets the impression that educators dare not rely on this way of putting it, for fear that young couples may use love as a justification and never mind the ceremony. So the message that chastity is not a question of following rules but of caring enough about one relationship to say no to others where it is necessary comes across faintly too.

Instead a series of reasons are offered so blatantly self-interested that it is hardly surprising the teenagers pay no attention: 'He won't marry you if you do, parents say – i.e. hold out for a better price. 'Men don't like shop-soiled goods'

(*goods?*). 'Anyway you might get a baby' – which would make some sense if they were then told how not to – 'or V.D.' One can hardly say that a girl whose whole heart and senses tell her to love completely, and who then says 'No' because she might catch something, has been saved by morality.

But the theory is that if the young aren't kept out of each other's beds at all costs, their marriages will be shallow and temporary, the fabric of society will collapse and untended children will roam the streets. I believe the opposite to be the case. A tremendous concentration on the evils of premarital sex, if anything, *lessens* the chances of people staying clear of adultery. The sigh of relief that went up a week or two ago, when it was revealed that only about a quarter of teenagers had sexual experience, took no account of earlier marriage. Couples that race to the altar as soon as they are nubile are certainly more likely to be virgin when they get there, but not necessarily more likely to have made marriages they can and will stick to.

If people are given a rule that has no sense to it, prohibiting both sex before marriage and sex outside it, they will reject both pieces of advice; but if parents concentrated on building up the ideal of a faithful marriage, their children just might pay some attention. And I don't think Kinsey's findings, that those who sleep around before marriage also do so after, are as significant as they sound: where the taboo works equally against both, people have less chance of distinguishing between experiment, good or bad, and disloyalty.

Some people would say that the ideal of lining up feelings and actions is no help when it comes to marriage; or put it another way and ask how you can possibly promise to love someone for ever. You can't, of course. But what you are really promising at the altar is to *behave as if you did*. This means that in any conflict between two loves, you are already committed to deciding in favour of the one you married; if you regard physical love as a strengthening thing, you will continue to strengthen your marriage with it, and not cart some of it away to strengthen something else. For if you have been brought up to the sort of integrity we are talking about, the idea of a quick blow 'to get it out of your system' is nonsense: only the people who feel the whole thing is trivial or dirty find it easier to shrug off someone with whom they have shared the shame.

And in practice I wouldn't say fidelity works at all badly – in fact I'd say the alternative works a darned sight worse. (I am always being told of the advantages of adultery by people who have just been, or are about to be, divorced.) I think the people who can be genuinely unjealous of someone *whom they love* going to bed with someone else are at least as rare as, possibly rarer than, the people who only want to go to bed with the person they married. What is not rare at all is people who aren't much in love any more, or don't particularly care about physical love one way or the other, or who have got their physical and emotional feelings hopelessly divorced. To them I don't suppose adultery does much harm. Still, we can fly a bit higher than that.

Auden's poem puts it thus:

> *To lovers as they lie upon*
> *Her tolerant enchanted slope . . .*
> *Grave the vision Venus sends*
> *Of supernatural sympathy*
> *Universal love and hope*

But goes on to say:

> *Certainty, fidelity*
> *On the stroke of midnight pass*
> *Like vibrations of a bell.*

What you say when you marry someone is that they will

not pass, dammit; you are going to see that they don't. You say that you will swap the chance of finding a new love, here and now, once and for all, for the chance of going on feeling this one. The Rev. Geoffrey Bellhouse once described faith not as accepting a series of blind dogmas but as 'living your life on the evidence of your highest moments'. Lovers in their highest moments know they can build a life on it – and on this basis being unfaithful is an exact description of adultery.

There are two good reasons why I think we are going to have to drop this emphasis on virginity and concentrate on refurbishing the idea of a loving and faithful marriage. The first is that the logical end of the cheerfully adulterous marriage is the marriage of convenience. If physical love is not something I have exclusively with this woman, a man may say, then what is it we share? The house, the children; she does my shirts, I pay the housekeeping; the set-up, not the person. So why not fix the thing to get the best set-up in the first place? Settle the thing on the basis of shirt-ironing, not romantic enthusiasm? Then we can each go our separate ways, enjoying the deep, deep peace of the double bank-account, without tiresome jealousies, without ugly scenes – and without, to my mind, the best that two people can achieve together. Suzanne Lilar, in her book *Aspects of Love*, points out that this comes hardest on the woman: 'She brings to marriage her desire for the absolute, and is only required to run her house well.'

And the other reason is that the woman of many lovers, the man of many mistresses is, in the end, alone. You go off the rails once, you are still a married person with a married sex-life. You do it again, and again, you get involved with some, brush off others, and recover from each – then you have not *our* sex life, but *my* sex life. It is up to you to jostle the different claims, manipulate the different emotional holds

148

the affairs may have on you, and return in the end to – not *us*, but *me*. No one can be both half of an exclusive pair and also half of several other pairs; and few of us want to be that much alone.

Wayland Young says we should stop saying 'Sex is bad unless . . .' and start saying 'It is good except . . .'. I think we should simply say 'Sex is at its best when . . .'. Someone once said to me that adultery was unavoidable in hot countries: it was simply a question of climate; but a wiser friend immediately countered 'It isn't climate, it's whether'. Whether we keep our marriages strong is what matters most.

36 · Living Without Sex

In getting to the world's top female job, it seems to me that Indira Gandhi has a double edge in the competition. To start with she's a Nehru, which is always the most important thing about that family, overriding minor differences of sex and temperament; but she also has the advantage of being a widow, so that she need neither trip over her husband in the path of destiny nor be jeered at because she hasn't got one.

One would like to think, of course, that in this enlightened age the single woman had no social disadvantages to overcome. But I'm not sure things aren't getting worse in this respect and not better.

There are, for one thing, fewer and fewer of them. This is partly because there are more marriageable men around than before, partly because there's more money; but mainly because Freud and J. Walter Thompson between them have decreed that if you aren't successful at sex you aren't successful at anything.

Sex, they say, must be the dominant drive in everybody's life. You would think that a casual glance at a busful of housewives – the Cabinet – the W.I. – the Rotary – would make them think twice about the idea: do they *look* as if their lives were governed by sexual passion? Yet the single woman is supposed to be out of it just because hers can't be.

You can't be happy, it says here, without sexual fulfilment. These women *are* happy? Very well then, they are sleeping with their lapdogs, with Beelzebub, with each other. The generation that says we should strain our tolerance (not to say credulity) to include those who sleep with apes and peacocks apparently cannot take the idea of people who sleep with nobody; or even of people who would rather sleep with nobody than sleep with the wrong ape.

One knows so well the incidental irritations of this viewpoint. You sit up half the night listening to the wails of some jilted bachelor, only to hear a casual bystander say, next day, that, so old and so unmarried, he must be queer. Not a psychological work that doesn't owlishly repeat that Lesbian couples are not frowned on in our society, since pairs of single women live openly together – rather missing the point that only those with absolutely one-track minds ever think they are Lesbians at all. I often wonder what the real Lesbians think about this unwarranted swelling of their ranks.

And a woman I know who has been interviewing a number of single women says she finds the ones under forty are all nervously anxious to tell her about their sex life as soon as she gets in the door, for fear she should think they don't have one.

What is so maddening about this tendency to see hormones in stones, crooks in the running brooks and sex in everything is that it gets in the way of so many other human affections.

The great Victorian family may have harboured an occasional Mr Barrett in its midst, but anyway the rest could rely straightforwardly on having cousins and uncles to love at least. But for people who see Freud not only under every bed but under every desk and armchair as well, all friendly contacts patterned on *other* family relationships, on feelings of fathers for sons, mothers for anything weak, aunts for small nephews, sisters for sisters, become shrunk to this single idea.

The result of it can be that people on their own are cut off by sheer self-consciousness from a whole lot of deep human contacts – enough of which might make them scarcely notice that they *were* alone in the marital sense.

I suppose you could say that a woman who thinks she is

better off single (or who simply finds herself single and makes a good job of it) shouldn't bother one way or the other what anyone thinks about it; but I think this is naïve. People always are sustained or hurt by what others think of them.

The generation of splendid spinsters now nearing retiring age may have lived in single cussedness as far as general opinion was concerned; but the people who mattered to them thought of them as pioneers, as people proving something of value about woman's freedom; the wives in the bridge club may have thought they were missing something but at least the feeling was mutual. But of today's generation of girls well over ninety per cent will get married, which means in effect that they are growing up without a serious celibate alternative, which presumably goes (aren't mathematics wonderful) for the men, too. I think it's a pity.

Look at all those men who live for their work – all those wives (ask any social worker) whose attitude to sex is 'My husband's very good – he doesn't bother me much'; the dedicated tea-cosy women who can shed light through a whole hostel of refugees; the men whose talent for domesticity, for giving a woman enough emotion to live on, is just about zero; what are we doing by making them feel they have to be hitched at all costs?

Of course, the theory is that we'll get psychology, chromosomes, baby care and housing so streamlined that everyone will grow up a perfect mate – but is it likely?

In the Middle Ages, you could be a nun; in the last century a quarter of the population never got married at all; a number of advanced civilizations have got that way partly by offering to those who were better at something else an honoured alternative to mating. If ours is ceasing to do so, it will be the narrower for it. Pigeon-holing people is always a clumsy policy, especially if the hole has another pigeon in it already.

37 · Banks – I

No one will be surprised that the banks have chosen a set of reforms uniquely convenient to them and inconvenient to the public. They want to open a little longer on weekdays; there will be twenty-four hours more time to catch up with a crooked cheque and no Saturday opening. The only benefit that most of us will get from these plans is that we need no longer be sneered at on Saturdays. The only thing that would really make life easier for us – longer opening hours, shorter queues at lunchtime and detailed statements – would involve taking on more bank staff; and this they have firmly decided not to do.

They say, of course, that they find it difficult to recruit as it is. But they also say that the average age of their female staff is fifteen to twenty-three: what about the returning married women, who positively thrive on shift working? No mention of them. And look what they offer their female staff anyway. For bright boys they advertise a career that opens up the prospect of being a manager by the time they are thirty. But for girls they offer the bait of being typists and clerks – not the way to urge girls to make banking a career. It could be, too, that the stuffiness of their image is against them in recruiting anyway. Banks like to think they are as solid and unchanging as their marble porticos; but they are nothing of the kind. A bank will bounce a cheque and close the account of one over-drawn man, but send nothing worse than a gentle reproof to another equally broke. They add up their bank charges with the help (or so it seems) of a horoscope, an abacus and a bent pin.

They reject as unsafe the idea of keeping one bank per district open on a Saturday for cashing small cheques, yet do just this at airports, where presumably the getaway conditions are ideal – though *The Times* blew the gaff on this when it said selective opening would not work 'from the point of view of competition between rival banks'.

The banks' moral attitudes seem as inflexible as granite when you meet them head on; but in fact they go up and down with the state of the Bank rate. A friend of mine who used to be a farmer said that what he loathed most about his bank was the way they would urge you to borrow when the Government said the nation was doing fine, and then, if the Government changed their mind, made you feel a moral weakling for having done so. They forget it is not the state of the nation that determines your needs but the state of you; and that it does not suddenly become irresponsible folly to want a roof over your five children just because the Bank rate has gone up.

What they really enjoy, of course, is being Authority. They may not have God behind them but by Heaven they have the Bank of England; and like all petty tyrants they take it out on those least able to resist. Who is likelier to let them down, a flash businessman or a salaried wretch who wants a tenner till next Tuesday? The former, obviously – but you can guess who the bank will favour.

I remember during my ill-fated stay at Roedean we had little cheque books, in which we wrote under the stony glare of our schoolmistresses: the atmosphere was quite as much a preparation for financial life as the cheques themselves.

And there is not much you can do to fight back. You can write frivolous cheques: A. P. Herbert's bank teases include writing one on an egg, and his character Haddock landed himself in a Misleading Case by writing his income tax cheque on the side of a white cow and herding it towards the Inland

Revenue. A friend of mine once wrote 'Pay this horrible person . . .' and the bank told her that to get the money she must endorse it 'this horrible person'. My father has added 'Dammit' or 'And not a penny more' to cheques he regretted writing. But possibly the only final thing you can do is to leave, and I'm surprised people don't do it more. We have done it twice so far: the first time I left a bank was because they asked me what a certain cheque, with a male signature, was *for*: they may be allowed to do this for tax reasons, but they made it sound as if I'd slept for it.

The second time was when, after having a healthy balance for eleven years (my husband's, not mine, I need hardly say) the bank could offer nothing towards our housing problem but the name of a mortgage company.

Leaving may achieve little, but it does at least remind you that these creatures are not your father in God or your head-master, but a set of traders in stiff collars who make a good thing out of handling your – repeat *your* – money.

Bank trade will not be increased by the reforms: on the contrary. But the trade of those places – hairdressers, clubs, grocers – who now do the bank's work for them by cashing cheques at convenient hours will, I prophesy, go up. I propose, in readiness for the new deal, to see just how long I can keep going on these and a Post Office Savings book without ever going anywhere near the bank – months probably.

In fact, I suppose after this article I will have to stay away anyhow.

38 · Banks – II

Not since the last time I inadvertently trod on the cat's tail have I heard such a squawk of rage as I got out of the anguished banks after my article on them three weeks ago. Indeed, had it not been for the rich, approving purrs of their customers, I should by now be cowering behind sackcloth, ashes and a nervous twitch.

On one thing, however, I must apologize. The banks are *not* stuffy, they are *not* like headmasters: no headmaster could do such a crisp line in invective as bankers when roused. 'One-sided, vacuous and distorted article . . .', 'infantile peevishness . . .', 'splenetic outburst . . .', 'definitely intended to attract that section of the public hitherto devoted to the *News of the World* . . .', 'naïveté and complete immaturity of extreme youth. . . .' One offered to give me the address of a good pawnbroker; my favourite said that if I earned my living as a journalist, it would be unsafe to advance me even ten pounds; and one confirmed just about everything I was complaining about when he questioned 'the arrogant assumption that bank services should be suited to her personal requirements'.

On the other hand, we had a lot of fresh evidence from the aggrieved public. The banks' contention that they refuse loans for only very good reason seems belied by the experience of a decorator who, contract and securities in hand, was refused a bridging loan for a big job of work; when she finally got her fee, the bank said to let them know if she ever wanted help.

Women seem particularly bitter about banks; perhaps because they are treated worse, perhaps because their financially cautious husbands won't back them up in a row. Sir Stanley Unwin reminded me of his experience some years ago when he opened two identical accounts for his infant daughter; he paid into one and his wife or his governess paid into the other. He was treated perfectly; but after six months the two women felt so humiliated that they refused to go back. One woman was irritated by the way they always sent the statement of the joint account – to which she contributed as much as her husband – privately to him alone: another was embarrassed, on opening an account, by having to sign with the bank clerk a statement that he had explained bank procedure to her and she 'appeared to understand'; she didn't feel any better about it when they made a mistake of £1,000 in the account shortly after. 'And whatever mistakes they make,' wrote one man bitterly, 'they *never, never* apologize' – unless you threaten to leave.

This, of course, works better if you have a big balance, or even a big overdraft, to remove. One college official said the bank told him curtly to get rid of his overdraft; when he proposed getting rid of it by moving it across the street, they grovelled, apologized and even halved their excessive charges.

On this question of charges, I had a revealing letter from a man who had worked in a bank for twenty-two years. 'The trick very often consists of overcharging the customers without a marked business sense, i.e. the wealthy widow or the small trader who maintains but a modest balance. These are milked for many guineas, which should justly be charged to difficult customers with active accounts, but who refuse to pay more than the minimum bank charge.' This would explain, I suppose, the woman asked to pay thirty-three and a half per cent charges on her overdraft.

Perhaps, for the record, I should clear up one confused point about Why We Left Our Bank – it wasn't a mortgage we wanted out of them, it was a possible bridging loan and some sympathy: we got neither. This bank used to address my husband as Pilot Officer, not only ten years after he left the Air Force, but ten years after he became Flying Officer, anyway; and this is not an irrelevance: they seemed to regard all ex-officers, however conscripted, as being equally unreliable. We now do fine at the District, where they not only treat you like a human being but have the Beatles' bank balance behind them.

I must admit that I did have a lot of letters from satisfied customers – of the Co-operative Wholesale Society Bank. They charge a flat five shillings a statement page, pay interest on the current account and allow you to cash cheques at Co-op shops in ordinary shop hours; the head office is at 99 Leman Street, E.1. The Trustee Savings Bank often stay open for longer hours, and the Mayfair London Bank Limited (70 Park Lane, W.1) stay open from nine in the morning till ten at night even at week-ends. One reader keeps *four* savings bank books, so that he can take out forty pounds at a time – surely enough for anyone.

The banks want to roast *me* alive; a lot of people obviously want to roast *them* alive; and what all this anger proves, it seems to me, is that whatever right the banks have on their side, they are just not getting it across to the paying customers. The bank manager, to the public, is the one with a glass eye in the story: you could tell which it was because it had the kindlier expression. The screen of discretion and secrecy behind which they prefer to work is doing more harm than good.

No doubt there are two sides to the question, as to the counter: but the marble-and-brass barrier was put there by the banks. It's up to them to come across it – if *we* try to crash it, we just get arrested.

39 · Down With Skool

Dear Hazel,

Thank you for your letter inviting me to contribute to the Roedean Development Fund. I must say I am surprised that, in the circumstances, I count as an Old Girl, but your letter certainly brought back memories. I could almost hear the school song in my ears as I read it: a song, you may remember, taken without emendation from Harrow all about the tramp of the twenty-two men (though I suppose if anyone *had* become the tramp of twenty-two men, she'd have been expelled).

The Roedean you and I were at was not, of course, typical. Evacuated to the Lake District, we were harangued by the Head from a pulpit in a Methodist chapel, forced by wartime shortages to have icicles *inside* the windows and our eiderdowns *inside* the sheets; and our formative years were spent among the Edwardian splendours of the Keswick Hotel.

A feature of this that I remember was a staircase lampstand in the form of a Negress eight feet high. My father once mortified me by slapping it on its polished flank, saying, 'Distinguished old girl, I suppose.'

The hotel's main advantage from my point of view, however, was a large relief map of the district, which enabled me to plot in some detail the route I would take when, after two years, I finally bicycled away.

The school, to do it credit, was extremely decent about this incident: it required no fees in lieu of notice and even offered to take me back – though this courtesy, as my husband points out, is also extended by H.M. Prisons. And they were a pretty good school from the teaching point of view. The trouble was that it was all at an intellectual level: contact with teachers as human beings was entirely prevented by the knowledge that you would be thought a filthy little sneak if you were seen talking to them.

I admit that a lot of what was wrong was wrong with me: I came from a different school and a different background and had the wrong green uniform of the one, the wrong pink politics of the other. I was so bad at games that they finally gave up trying to teach me; and since in every class there has to be a fat girl who cannot in any circumstances be got over the horse in one heave, the fat girl was, of course, me. And I couldn't take teasing. Looking back on it, I feel better about being teased – it gives one a cosy martyred glow – than about what inevitably followed: I became, as soon as I got half a chance, a bully myself.

At this point, Hazel, you are probably saying that I am wildly overstating it: that even one who, like myself, lost a stone a term from sheer misery must have had *some* bright moments. And of course I did. But they shed no light on the surrounding gloom, and it has taken me years to work out why: I think it was the sense of captivity. Never at any point in the twenty-four hours at boarding school are you free – free of the school, of the other girls' opinions, of the stiff-upper-lip ruling that prevented some girls who were just as unhappy as I was even telling their parents they were miserable. This is the poison gas of boarding schools that Gwen Raverat smells whenever she goes back to one: once smelt, never forgotten.

Still, I realize that not everyone feels like that. The reason you are not, I am afraid, going to get your cheque is not that the toughening process makes the odd girl miserable but that I can't see any point in toughening up girls like this at all. The boys' public schools (not that I hold any special brief for *them*) do make some sort of sociological sense: you take the youths at puberty away from their mothers' softening influence, you give them tough exercises to make them strong warriors and to keep their minds off sex (it says here), you give them a glorious games hierarchy to fight their way up and at the end of it they have been through an initiation. They have no doubt of their identity as British, upper-middle-class, and male. But how can you possibly apply the same tribal techniques to girls, who have the opposite things to learn?

Take, as one classic instance, the boarding school attitude to illness. One house matron is tough: no good going to her because you felt too frightful for cricket practice before breakfast. Another is more sympathetic – and the chances are she is regarded as 'soft'. Yet which are women supposed to be – good at comforting the sick, or good at spotting malingerers, like a sergeant-major?

Well, well, it's all past history now. I am sure that, back in Sussex, it is very different these days; it is years now since I woke from my commonest nightmare of dreaming I was back there. But I must confess it will be all one to me if the jolly old school, far from developing, falls off the Rottingdean cliffs into the sea.

Yours,

Katharine.

L

40 · The New Labour Movement

You can hardly pass a book-stall these days without seeing, among the nudies and the nonsense, a half-naked woman giving either birth or suck to her young. The next one you shy away from – and the newest out – may be *What Every Woman Needs to Know About Childbirth* (Heinemann) by Prunella Briance and Grantly Dick-Read's widow, Jessica.

They represent what you might call the Unreformed Church of the cheerful childbirth cult; for the movement has many manifestations. Grantly Dick-Read started it in the twenties with the emphasis on relaxation and telling women what was going on within; he was dead against routine pain-killers and said that a fully natural birth should be painless anyway. Then came psycho-prophylaxis, brought back from Russia by the French doctor Fernand Lamaze in 1951; he (and his disciple, 'Painless Pierre' Velay) taught a specialized form of breathing, pooh-poohed the Dick-Read methods as mere mysticism, but still roundly asserted that women felt pain only because they'd been conditioned to expect it.

What the National Childbirth Trust (which was originally the Natural Childbirth Trust, founded by the same Prunella Briance in 1956) now teaches is not the straight Lamaze method but an adaptation of it. The Natural people gleefully point out that they have abandoned Lamaze's extra oxygen, and the rest of the world notes that they no longer promise a painless labour. Erna Wright's book, *The New Childbirth* (Tandem Books), embodies their teaching; but clear as these distinctions of theory are to the theorists themselves, there are plenty of women whose view on childbirth is an optimistic cocktail of the lot.

In any case, it takes more than knocking the word 'natural' out of the title to clear out the cranks inevitably attracted by the word – and a pregnant crank is an awesome thing. For those who have been told that it is only civilization, drugs, and doctors that stop women dropping their babies as casually as greengages, Dr Anthony Barker's splendid book *The Man Next Me* (Fontana) is a salutary corrective. He writes about his medical work in Zululand, where large numbers of babies die for lack of drugs and doctors; where the only people (apart from natural childbirthers) who think that primitive woman springs up with a glad cry as soon as the cord is cut are the white farmers who want her back at work directly; and where one is irresistibly reminded of the ardent English-women who put down any setback or depression to 'the wrong attitude' by the hideous old gamps who sit round the labouring Zulu ascribing every hold-up to a failure in courage. It makes you wonder whoever started this idea that nature was so trouble-free: *nature* doesn't care if a woman has thirty babies, of whom only ten survive. It is civilization that expects every pregnancy to end in a fit, well-adjusted school leaver.

Setting aside the hoo-ha, however, the method has a great deal to recommend it. It is obviously better that a woman should know what is going to happen to her than that she should crawl into the labour ward trembling with terror; and the breathing exercises can be an enormous help, especially to those who are lucky enough to have a pretty easy time of it anyway (me for one).

Unfortunately, like so many medical improvements, it can have unfortunate side effects. One is that, in conditioning a woman away from the idea of automatic agony, it is easy to give her such rose-coloured hopes that she feels completely let down if things are difficult. A cousin of mine was the star of her preparation class, but had a deep transverse arrest (i.e. baby stuck sideways quite far back). Naturally, the birth was neither painless nor unaided. Next morning her instructor came round and said: 'Well, you *were* a disappointment to us' – it took her weeks to get over her sense of failure. And another girl I know confessed to feeling beforehand (as I bet most of the prepared do feel) faintly superior to anyone so unenlightened as to have had a hard labour; she was completely shattered when her own hurt badly, and spent days apologizing for having 'made such a fuss'. 'I couldn't understand these unprepared mothers who screamed the place down and then came out with their babies half an hour later grinning all over their faces,' she said.

The more sensible practitioners do try to get away from this idea of 'success' or 'failure'. But while those who come through correctly preen themselves on their achievement, those who have had it tough will go on feeling they have let the side down; and you will still get the ludicrous situation of a woman who has produced a healthy baby saying she has 'failed' in labour.

The object of the exercise, after all, was to produce a *baby*. And this is, I think, the far more serious criticism that can be levelled at the new labour movement: that they make having a child seem a process that is nine months long instead of fifteen years. The N.C.T. give nine lectures: of these, only one is about care of the baby, all the rest are about Mum's Great Moment. Yet the average woman in England is only in labour for perhaps thirty-six hours in her whole lifetime. An obstetrician puts it like this: 'We are desperately short of good parents; in ante-natal classes you've got a captive audience – perhaps it's the only moment when these women are really receptive. And what do we do? We teach them to breathe.'

There is no doubt that some women make a fetish of the labour itself, to the point where they almost forget what it is

164

all about. A doctor told me he once had a terrific struggle to save the baby of a woman who was dead set on resisting forceps – even although the baby had its cord round its neck. And one of the leading childbirther's first words to a newly delivered friend of mine were not 'How's the baby?' but 'Did you have gas?'

I would be prepared to bet that a woman who has had a lousy labour and forgets about it is in a better way towards being a good mother than the woman still obsessed with her own performance in the labour ward, good or bad. I am all for the method; but from the people who make the wedding seem the marriage, the door the house, and the labour the child's whole upbringing, good Lord deliver us – with gas-and-oxygen if necessary.

41 · The Craft of Husbandry

In that nostalgic primer of the early thirties, *The Perfect Hostess*, there is a page headed 'What Every Husband Ought to Know'. Some of it has a fine period flavour: 'How to mend the electric bells; How to mark out the tennis court.' Some of it is only too timeless: 'How to put a washer on a tap; How to be nice when you have made a perfect fool of yourself.' But a bigger and better primer for the modern husband would clearly fill a long-felt want (I don't know why that always sounds like a Christmas stocking).

I fancy marriage is more taken up with demarcation disputes than it was in the thirties; the mere fact that men are occasionally landed with women's jobs has produced a whole new set of masculine evasion techniques. They know the art of doing enough washing-up to be thanked without going to absurd lengths (like washing saucepans) of actually getting it finished – and the fact that this is also used by women and charwomen in their struggle for ascendancy only proves how efficient it is.

Husbands have also perfected a means for getting the maximum moral credit out of their occasional pieces of parent-craft. The trick is first to make a virtue of necessity by offering as an extravagant gesture to do any chore which seems to be coming their way anyway; and thereafter to tread a delicate tight-rope of martyrdom.

For if *he* makes too much fuss about getting up with the baby one morning a week, *she* can claim six times the martyrdom for doing it every day; but let the effort go unremarked and she might actually think he didn't suffer. Skilled performers do a kind of Battle-of-Britain understatement, akin to Danny Kaye's 'Just a scratch – I set the bones myself'.

With the decline of clubs and the female encroachment of pubs the modern husband needs, too, some advanced skills for ever being on his own without causing offence – or at least causing a stream of little cups of coffee and inquiries whether he wants anything from the shops. Women, though remarkably good at doing not much, are rotten at doing nothing and can't bear to see it being done: so it is essential to get out of sight before you start. One man in *Ordinary Families* built his house at the other end of Suffolk because he reckoned the only time a married man gets to himself is in the train going to work. Men with a study and a set of taboos to defend it can always say they are working ('I concentrate better with my eyes shut'). Some men go to ground in the bathroom, taking an unconscionable time a-drying; others buy dogs for the sole purpose of taking them for walks on which 'Here, boy!' is the only conversational effort required.

When it comes to escaping from one's wife, there is an old bachelor rule which husbands seem to find a great help played in reverse. Bachelors of sense make a point of not asking a girl out on the same night each week, because it is so much harder to say, 'I'm not taking you out next Saturday' than simply to lengthen the interval between a whole lot of assorted Fridays and Tuesdays. Similarly a firm habit of being out one night a week gets quickly accepted (she can always put her hair in curlers and dream herself niece to 'The Man from Uncle'), whereas intermittent evenings on parole need a new justification every time.

For the more difficult task of escaping the things she wants you to do, husbands who have not succeeded in classifying all jobs, including digging the turnips, as women's work have a hard time of it. My impression is that schoolmasters and writers score best: they seem to manage to alternate 'Don't bother me with it now, I'm working' with 'Do we have to spoil the holidays with *that*?' almost indefinitely. If men turn a deaf ear to pleas about the gas bill long enough, few wives have the stamina to wait until it is cut off before they pay it themselves.

But when it comes to deaf ears, men need a selective mechanism. Just as a woman can pick up a baby's cry while oblivious of the noise of the washing machine, the radio and her own singing, so a husband needs a sixth sense that will pick up anything important from the general stream of female chatter (women are endowed with an ability to talk when no one is listening so that they can teach their children to speak; on males it has the opposite effect).

Any fool can nod absently when his wife is talking, but then he is absolutely shattered when what she was warning him about actually happens. This goes particularly for warning signs of impending birthdays and anniversaries: there is a tale of a girl who broke off her engagement to a blond demigod because he forgot her birthday, and was later found blissfully married to a wizened and hideous historian whose only quality was his ability to remember dates.

The one thing no primer can tell you, of course, is how to avoid being blamed for the weather – not to speak of Communism, the non-delivery of letters and President Johnson's gall-stones. But at least if the problem can't be solved, it can be shared: for the motto 'Why keep a spouse and blame yourself?' is adopted at the moment of marriage by every human being alive. Indeed I can't think why they don't write it on the wedding cake in green sugar.

42 · How's the Old Complaint?

A man at dinner was harrowing his companion with the plight of some arctic explorers who found themselves marooned on an ice-floe. No food, no water, no means of signalling; there they were, floating hopelessly out to sea. 'But what did they *do*?' she twittered.

He considered. 'They complained,' he said.

Those men must have experienced an extreme form of a trouble we all have. We know in this consumer-conscious decade that we are supposed to make a fuss, to stand up for our rights and to complain; but *how*?

Half the time we get it all wrong. We get so angry that people can't hear what we say; or we suffer from H. G. Wells's disorder; 'I always get so amiable when I *meet* a man,' or we just grumble and let things slide. Somehow we seldom manage to resemble the Just Consumer, striding about getting value for money without even raising his voice. So I have been asking around among the complained at as well as the complaining to see if there are any techniques that really work.

Some things are generally agreed. It's no good wasting your rage on the waiter or the shop-girl, who can't do anything even if they wanted to; go to the *maître d'hôtel* or to the buyer and, if they're no help, to the manager. One man, who on two visits about a bad pair of sandals got nothing but rudeness from the shoe-shop, got his money back plus postage when he sent them up north to head office. And the last time we complained about putrescent fish in a restaurant we later heard that, ours being only one of many, the chef had been

169

moved on – though my boss was furious: 'While he was there we could avoid him,' he said. 'Now we don't know *where* he's working.'

It's a great mistake, too, to think you strengthen your case by overstating it. If you say you've worn a blouse twice when you've had it a couple of months, you simply class yourself with the people who really do try to get a new carpet by complaining of an old cigarette burn (even the consumer watchdogs admit that well over half of consumer complaints aren't justified). You should resist the urge, too, to say too much in your letter. Sarcasm doesn't help, and the blow-by-blow account – 'At 2.21 the manageress was still out at lunch' – only obscures the central point; it makes it easier, too, for them to write you off as one of nature's fireworks: they set light to your paper and retire.

When I asked which complaints were dealt with quickest, one and all replied, 'The polite ones' – which I'd have believed more completely if they had first honestly said, 'The ones from friends of the chairman.' Any sort of pull helps – bring in your M.P. if you are complaining of a public body, since they dread questions in the House worse than scabies; bring in the trade organization, if there is one; if even your deceased wife's sister is a journalist or the manager's babysitter or the head of a noisy consumer group, pull her in, too.

The fact that they did all beg for courtesy, though, was interesting; and set me wondering if we often don't work out sufficiently what we want from a complaint. For if we did, we'd realize that often getting it off your chest and getting your money back are *alternatives*. Short of a court case, your only real hope is to get someone in the organization on your side; yet we often use, with people we have a grievance against, techniques which in any other circumstances we would know perfectly well wouldn't work. The trader, in his own eyes, is doing no harm to anyone when suddenly an outraged woman rushes at him and says, 'You're a thief and a villain and I want you to go out of your way to help me'; it's hardly surprising he doesn't. Oh, sure, I know we are in the *right* – but that isn't the point.

Of course there are traders with whom niceness gets nowhere, and you may as well try losing your temper; but here women are at a disadvantage. No woman likes to picture herself as a screaming virago, and it seems to me that the only way you can cause maximum consternation while keeping that feminine image they all urge us to preserve is to burst into tears – I'd say faint, if the floors were cleaner. Then the Englishman's horror of a scene (which works against you when you want your husband to complain) works suddenly in your favour: tears can act on some truculent little functionary like lemon drops on an oyster.

Well, who is the happy grumbler, who is he? I see him as a man eight feet tall, with a bowler hat and a greying moustache; he has an upper-class accent, is not accustomed to being contradicted and all his charge accounts are marked with a red X meaning 'Watch it!' In other words, a retired Army officer, with an air of authority and plenty of time to persist. Superficial good manners only thinly disguising an underlying hardness is the winning combination.

The rest of us usually have it, alas, the other way round: a hard crust round a quaking jelly, like a bad flan. And our dignity disintegrates at a touch. The last time I acted in the spirit of the great consumer movement, I walked out of a restaurant where they were being rude to me with the fine words, 'I'm not sure you can serve me anything if that's your attitude.' But as I reached the door a sarcastic voice said: 'And could we have back the spoon your baby is carrying?'

43 · Mo'ther (mŭdh-), n.1.
Female Parent

Ever since the man defined ambidextrous as not letting your right hand know who is holding your left, abstract nouns have been a standing temptation to writers. Perhaps the biggest killing was made by the Peanuts people, with their book *Happiness is a Warm Puppy*; they have now moved on to *Love is Walking Hand in Hand*, and I see no reason why they should ever stop. No reason, either, why they should have the field to themselves: I propose to make a corner in 'motherhood' while there is yet time.

Motherhood is the art of doing things with one hand; motherhood is the art of hiding *Little Red Riding Hood* after the eighteenth reading. Motherhood is leapfrog conversation, intelligible only to other mothers: it goes, 'I don't think it's so much that he's wrong in don't go near the edge, dear principle as that he's so terrible put it *down* at the practice.'

Motherhood is finding a piece of sausage in your purse; motherhood is finding your purse in the dustbin; motherhood is not finding your purse.

Motherhood is visible: you can tell the age of the child by noting the position of those little white touches recommended by fashion: mothers with burpable babies have shoulders limed like statues with bird-droppings, those with older children have Farex on the hemline or poster-paint at the waist. Motherhood is a dead give-away: children scratch their scalps with a nail-file in careful imitation of mother; children even, when asked in the course of road training: 'What do we do when we want to cross the road?' have been known to say right in front of their fathers, 'Take a taxi?'

Motherhood is self-control: not laughing when they spit their food out at you, and not weeping when they spit their food out at you. Motherhood is growing up – you can't throw a scene at a baby and expect *him* to say, 'There, there, dear.' Motherhood is not knowing the young visitor's word for its potty; motherhood is a wet carpet.

Motherhood goes without transition from wondering if the little one will break to wondering *what* he'll break; from frenziedly remembering that microbes matter to knowing that hygiene is the art of the possible. Motherhood is extreme sensitivity of the ears, so that you can hear a baby crying through *Ready, Steady, Go* and a sewing-machine; and a merciful insensitivity of the nose, which leads one to suppose one's own baby doesn't smell. Motherhood, indeed, is fraught with illusion: the belief that the shoes will last another month, that these photographs anyway aren't boring, that the other child started it.

Motherhood is cowboys and Indians. Mothers, seeing the wigs and hairpieces on the counter, think first what lovely scalps they'd make, only second about their cosmetic value. In this game, only the corpses get a bit of rest. The phrase, 'The only good Indian is a dead Indian' was undoubtedly coined by a mother, playing Indian. Motherhood is having the moral edge on everybody except office cleaners and night-watchmen, since none but the Mums are up in time to bring the lark its early morning tea; motherhood is hating to put the clocks back since no one knows how to put back the children. Motherhood is bags under the eyes; motherhood is hell.

Motherhood is an unfair vulnerability, suddenly developed, to any picture or story of a child in trouble. Oxfam stories, which once got simply classified as 'How dreadful' along with

Rhodesia, remote earthquakes and the nation's teeth, can haunt mothers for days. Maybe this makes mothers tough: they know their weakness and don't leave it exposed.

Motherhood lets you in for being harangued by hags at parties if you don't breast-feed till the child sits its eleven-plus; it provokes madonna-emotions in some of the craggiest male breasts going: motherhood is full of surprises.

Motherhood is a mystique, seen from outside: to enter it is to walk with awe through the portals of a great cathedral and find yourself in a grubby workshop. Motherhood is extreme cynicism about words like Motherhood; but it breathes new life into other words and phrases: such as containing the offensive, what goes down must come up, and it's an ill wind that blows nobody any good.

Motherhood is also 4,587 other things, some of them even serious, and adequately dealt with in books like Spock and the Bible and *The Ascent of F 6*. They all agree, however, that motherhood is not a warm puppy.

44 · *Motherhood is a Flood of Letters*

Parenthood is a subject on which there are no experts: which is splendid, since it makes us all experts. A few weeks ago I wrote an article about Motherhood, and was immediately deluged by a rich shower of definitions from parents, written in that curious disjointed style that comes from having every sentence interrupted at least twice in the middle.

The Observer parent, it seems, is a bit like Flanders fields, across which waves of conflict sweep back and forth – and the fathers get it (or say they get it) quite as much as the mothers. Fatherhood, I was told, is shaving in the bathroom with a hangover and being asked 'Is God in here?' It is unwanted murals on a newly papered wall; it is arriving home exhausted to find one's hitherto elegant, orderly, understated pad covered to a depth of five inches with bricks, celluloid fish and Dinky toy cement mixers. It is dreaming of a quiet sit-down with the paper and finding your chair guarded by several little bodies hopefully clutching storybooks. It is hiding Mrs Tittlemouse after the seventy-ninth reading and producing it again after an unbelievable uproar.

Fatherhood is the five minutes between the breath-catching sight of a brand-new baby and the receipt of a letter saying, 'Term starts on September 15; fees are twenty-two guineas a term payable in advance.' It is saying at a party, 'Don't eat the sandwiches so fast, dear,' and hearing the ringing reply: 'But they're so *small*, Daddy.' It is trying to persuade your friends you don't, actually, want to go on the booze every single night while mother is in hospital having, guess what, another one; it is watching a child with a sparkler on Guy Fawkes night and feeling suddenly, surprisingly, sad. It is *Gatsby*, *Memoirs of a Foxhunting Man*, and *The Making of a President 1960*. And when it comes to potties, the male mind has the answer: there should be a British Standard word for it.

But mothers, understandably, got it off their chests most, and one of their definitions is just about a blanket for the lot: motherhood is going through experiences which, if it had been for science or the Girl Guides, would get you a medal. Such as living in acute discomfort in a tiny tent on a tiny island so that *they* can learn self-reliance, or travelling across France with a fourteen-month-old baby in the back of some-one else's car ('It has not made me a Better Person'); it is being handed an entire filthy set of football clothes at bedtime in the expectation that they will be clean and dry by the next morning – and the boots cleaned as well.

School-age children plainly make a whole battlefield of their own: one mother defined her state as wrestling with Caesar's belligerent excursions while one's husband is gnash-ing his teeth because supper isn't ready. It is discovering that a box of 500 saccharines, when spilt, contains 3,847 tablets. It is not being strong-minded enough to let mice, rabbits, cats and ponies die of periodic neglect. But the ones who had opted for boarding-school fared no better: it is getting exas-perated, they said, by untidy bedrooms and mess all over the house and then suffering the empty agony of empty beds in immaculately tidy rooms.

And both sorts had a fair time of it with medical problems: buckets of blood, broken bones, burnt fingers and dirty grazes; calling a doctor to a child with a temperature of 104 degrees who is sitting up smiling by the time the doctor arrives, and not calling a doctor for fear of incurring his wrath while the child's appendix bursts. And they could never work out whether it was the start of polio or just the start of

Wednesday – shades of Betty Macdonald's 'Ann was at home with a sore throat and/or history test'.

They were philosophical: motherhood is resignation, motherhood is the conviction you are a failure as a mother. Motherhood is fair shares – letting the other mothers have equal time to descant upon their offspring (and not just saying at the school sports as your own bounds off to the changing-room: 'Now we have to watch a lot of unnecessary children jump'). Motherhood is never being right, as one mother put it, or, according to another, accepting that you know nothing at all about anything while being expected to know all about everything and be able to do anything. It is having to be interested in everything from books to Bartok. Motherhood is standing back and letting them grow away from you. Motherhood is pretending to trust boys with real guns and girls with real young men.

And one or two managed to be lyrical about it – 'It is waking up with a warm rosy suckling'; 'It is watching five children up to their necks in the moonlit Atlantic dipping their toothbrushes in the sea.' This was more than I had managed to be – for which one reader ticked me off roundly and another got so gloomy about the whole prospect that she practically broke off her engagement.

It is always hard to mention happiness without sounding like a woman's magazine: much easier to describe the way one's husband says, 'Wot, now?' when asked to mend a fuse than to outline the electricity of his personality, and a good deal simpler to record how much it costs to have a small wooden pig removed from the bowels of one's typewriter than to describe how you feel when your baby dances along a sunlit beach wearing nothing but a hat.

Not one of the readers mentioned the nutritious qualities of country margarine, the germs beyond the S-bend or the whiteness of their kiddies' collars, so the people who write the

TV commercials may not have got it quite right about what *is* a Mum. But it is plainly a lot more than I had at first thought; as one reader put it: 'K. W. has experienced only the fringes of motherhood and should prepare herself for much, much worse to come.' Not that it ends there, mind you: there was one who simply said: 'Just you wait till you're a grandmother!'

45 · The Glass of Fashion

In the fashion world, they are very good at justifying the changes. They explain earnestly that woolly skirts keep out the cold; and bare midriffs, they assure you, are good for ventilation. Out-of-fashion works hard at the same game: short skirts are absurdly chilly, and long ones trail in the cat saucers. Neither side comes out and says: 'It makes a change – and we hate or love it for that reason.' But for anyone who has ever worked in fashion, the amusing thing is to watch exactly the same process going on everywhere else.

Decoration, of course, hardly counts – it is so close to clothes. The up to date change from having stove burners and cookers one above the other and the children ranged in rows to having the parts of the cooker on the same level while the children are stacked in bunks. Streamlining, in which everything looks as if it is wrapped in warm ice-cream, is inevitably followed by brutalism, in which honest hard right-angles replace curves entirely – even for something like a record pickup that has to turn eight corners to avoid one curve. Osbert Lancaster recorded with glee the swing to elaborate Victoriana after the war, 'not the least enjoyable result of this latest development has been the forcing of the older generation, corduroy-clad, *New Statesman*-reading, Freud-reared, into a position of Barrett-like reaction'.

Nothing is sadder, of course, than to see advanced opinions abandoned by the tide like a distant sand-dune (when I read Angus Wilson's *Such Darling Dodos* I couldn't *believe* it was the progressive left-wingers he was getting at). But the booksy world is peculiarly subject to fashion. Look at poor Salinger, the toast of a decade, now like Omar turning down an empty Glass. Look at Eliot – why, I once had a pale young man on my doorstep say, 'You mean you don't go to Eliot for the things that really matter to you?' And when I was forced to admit that no, actually, I didn't, he vanished into the night. It couldn't happen now.

One would hardly expect the arts to be unmoved by fashion, though. Look at the way even titles come and go, from *Ode: Intimations of Immortality from Recollections of Early Childhood*, to *Jurgen* and *Cavalcade* and *Kangaroo*, back to *Oh Dad, Poor Dad, Mamma's hung you in the closet and I'm feelin' so sad* (I'm assured I'd be feeling a darned sight worse if I'd actually seen the play). Television does it; look at that trick of flashing a still photograph on the screen, witty when Braden first beat it out, now a cliché; or the Cinéma Vérité tendency not to see the face for the pores. Mass sociology goes in for collectives as studiously as the Ukraine, with its Persuaders, Status Seekers, Dream Makers: I know a drunken advertising man who is planning to round up the lot in a book called *The Sick-Makers*. Even the mating instincts of the art world tend to go in waves: I forget (for reasons of diplomacy) which literary figure it was who pointed out that in the thirties it was the thing to be queer and few had families; now, he said testily, you couldn't visit a single writer without getting jammed in the prams in the hall.

Family life, of course, is highly sensitive to the swing of fashion, since if there is one thing people react against, it's their parents; but expert advice pushes the thing along with gusto. Twenty-five years ago you potted a baby from the word go, but left its reading till three. Now (thanks partly to psychology but a good deal more to plastic pants) you don't pot the child for years and years but are allowed to teach it to read before it can walk. People used, too, to space their families, for a variety of good reasons; now the children hustle one another out of the bassinet as fast as it can be refilled – again for good reasons, but no one can ever remember off-hand what they are. Except for one woman I know who said plaintively: 'I know why psychiatrists advise you to have your children close together – more mothers go bonkers, it's good for trade.'

The L.S.E. goes from red to blue to pink; the steady state universe is not as steady as it used to be; Freudians and Jungians and Watsonians chase one another back and forth like armies in the Wars of the Roses. It is profoundly depressing to realize that no reform stays done, no discovery keeps its original blinding clarity. There is no truth so self-evident that it will not automatically find itself attacked in time – if only because it is so firmly accepted that no one can make a name for himself agreeing with it (all those youths who said, 'Very true, Socrates' – where are they now?). It takes more patience than most of us have got to sit back and wait for the enemy to go out of fashion, too; and it is no good just banging on the ceiling at the party of death and reaction going on in the room above.

The only thing, I think, is to resign yourself to the fact that you won't always be modern (or with it, or in, or, as dear old ladies in the little dress-shops put it, all the rage); but to make sure you get sick of things at your own rate. Mary Quant defined her fashion sense simply as 'I get tired of things quicker than other people' – this is the way to stay ahead. But throwing out everything unfashionable usually means tossing away Auntie's hideous tiara (value £10,000) as well; better abandon the effort to be in than to find yourself without that. The only things you can safely junk are trivialities, or the ones whose newness was their main appeal in the first place. That is, after all, what clothes are about – but not what anything else is.

Woman reveals herself in many ways, lest one good cos-

46 · Meeting Mary McCarthy
— A Profile

I knew Mary McCarthy by sight, I thought, as I waited for her in the Lanvin boutique: a severe-looking woman with a bun as she appears in the book-jacket photographs. Her appearance seemed to go well with the incisive writing, the ruthless criticism, the devastating analysis of female experience.

So when a great gawky American with loose grey curls under a large straw hat advanced towards me with a friendly, uncertain smile I simply didn't recognize her. It took me a long time to recover from the shock and fit the woman and the authoress together: to come to terms with this alarming youthfulness and reassemble my enormous admiration for her along different lines. That first morning, all I could do was yammer.

At Lanvin's, she was asking them to make up a piece of tribal cloth given her by an Underdeveloped friend; and on the whole they were taking it well. She was wearing a discreet navy dress they had made for her – with the success of *The Group* she bought couture for a season, but mostly she gets her clothes from the slightly less expensive boutique. It could not, however, be said that the effect was French: 'I hate the French uniform,' she said – and added such et ceteras as two-tone American shoes, a spotted scarf, a country hat.

Leaving Lanvin's, we dripped our way through the rain to Hermès next door: it's the world's most expensive leather shop, but surprisingly sells bathing dresses as well, and she bought one for a price that worked out at about a pound an inch. The bell rang; the shop shut for lunch; we were out on the street. 'That's it about the French,' she said as we climbed into a taxi. 'They *aren't* mercenary – they don't really want to sell you things at all. My son Reuel had the phrase for it: he said "Mummy, the French *grudge* gipping you".' She leant forward to give directions to the driver, and went on 'And what I hate about it is that you become so abject, you get so grateful to the one taxi-driver in a hundred that actually knows the way to where you want to go – and *he's* probably a foreigner.'

In a television programme some time ago she complained that the French never invite you to their homes; after which she received a number of sudden invitations. But she still maintains that most of the French people she likes have foreign wives or connections. Her husband, James West, with whom we lunched in the administrative château of O.E.C.D., where he works, thinks she overstates it; but they both prefer Poland to Paris. It was in Poland, where he was a diplomat and she was lecturing, that they originally met: one catches faint nuances of 'Darling, they're playing our country' whenever the place is mentioned.

I felt this later in the day when we climbed up the dark stairway to the studio of a Polish painter, Lebenstein, from whom they were to get a gouache. He provided champagne, but it did little to counteract the compelling melancholy of his paintings, each of which showed a more hopeless picture of life than the one before. When we finally tottered out I felt that the logical thing to do next would be to throw ourselves into the Seine, but the Wests cheered up at once. We whisked home through the rain to supper in their flat in the Rue de Rennes; it was an admirable supper, cooked from Elizabeth David, but it was not fattening. As she is a woman, and as she is an American, she was dieting.

A day so spent is not, apparently, typical: 'Mostly I don't do anything much except work,' she said. But the homes of those who really don't, look it – and hers didn't. It was pretty, very feminine: pale pink curtains she made herself, flowered wallpaper; lots of white paint against deep green, a pattern of hearts on the breeze curtains. The details were careful: a tiny rose in a minute bottle, a big butterfly in the disc of a glass, a Florentine miniature. In contrast, the kitchen was a spartan workroom: a stove specially got from Germany, and a big iron Spanish coffee-grinder: 'I found the electric grinder heats the coffee up; it isn't so good.'

She told me that Kay's flat in *The Group* – pillow ticking chair covers and red cushions – was one she had had in the thirties: 'It depresses me to see young people nowadays having exactly the same fads as we had, like absolute belief in psycho-analysis and absolute insistence on modern furniture.'

Her study was neat – Kenneth Tynan's denunciation of her article on Osborne was filed under Controversy – and her antique desk was dominated by a terrifying bird given her by the poet Robert Lowell; she works with it staring at her from a bare eight inches away, but says she hardly looks at it. She types all her own work – 'I hate to lose contact with the prime materials' – and uses the typewriter as a creative device: if she's stuck she starts typing out a bit she's sure of in the hope that the momentum will carry her over the sticky bit.

She usually works from nine till four, then goes out to shop for food. Her own lunch is something light – consommé or eggs, but never, I gathered, sloppy. 'I don't believe you should behave differently when you're alone and when you're with people,' she said. 'I suppose it's part of believing in singleness, not just doubleness.'

This shipshape discipline of her working life has been built up and maintained through some pretty fair private tempests. When she left Vassar, the New York women's college, and married her first husband she wasn't sure whether she wanted to be a writer or an actress. Her teachers at Vassar told her she'd never be any good at creative writing, 'and my husband saw me in a play and told me to forget about acting'.

For some time she wrote criticisms for small leftish magazines such as the *Partisan Review* – she was a Trotskyite and parted company with the Communists over the Moscow Trials of 1936. (Her anarchist sympathies could still be construed as leftish, but she has avoided the political arthritis you get if you try to maintain the same attitude for thirty years.) Then her extraordinary second husband, Edmund Wilson, 'put me in this little room and he didn't actually lock me in but it was clear I couldn't come out until I had written some fiction' – the first story in *The Company She Keeps*.

It took her seven years of steady trying to get free of Wilson, and she was then married for thirteen to Bowden Broadwater, a New York teacher who protected her and arranged their New York life around her 'as if I was a sort of precious writing machine'. She would show him each chapter as it was finished – not before, though she suspected he used to look; and now shows them to James West: 'Why *do* women writers have to show their work to someone?' She is now working on a book about a nineteen-year-old boy; one wonders if it will owe anything to her own son by Edmund Wilson, Reuel; but she isn't keen on talking about things before she has written them.

It was when she was sitting on a sofa with her feet under her, smoking continuously and talking about books, husbands, politics, people that the woman and the writer finally jelled, and I saw that the girlishness that had unnerved me at first was a vital part of the writer. I had always had the same feeling about her books: a horrified blend of 'This is so good everyone should read it' and 'Oh God, this is me all over – I hope *nobody* reads it'. I had never stopped to think that, if she had been as forbidding as I imagined, she could never have attracted the emotional experiences she dissects so devastatingly. Or, of course, the confidences: the books are not auto-biographical. She said she *impersonated* each person she wrote about: 'The Danish translator was the only one who spotted that *The Group* was written from the point of view of each girl in turn, like a pastiche.'

She confirmed, to my relief, my theory that the title is almost always the clue to her books: *The Company She Keeps* stresses the difficulty a woman on her own has in having any identity that is not just a reflection of each person she meets in turn; *The Group* is not just a random sample, but an exploration of the effect on these girls of thinking of themselves as a group of special people; *A Charmed Life* is what the intellectuals of New Leeds live, a life on special terms, out of all contact with reality: the girl loses it when she makes an actual real-life decision to take any sort of action, and is killed in a car crash.

Of her two great strengths as writer, one is certainly that she has opened up so many hitherto unmentioned areas of feminine experience. The contraception sequence in *The Group* is well known – 'That woman', said Sonnenberg, 'has done for the pessary what Herman Melville did for the whale'; since that book, too, people having trouble with breast-feeding can just say, 'Like Pris Hartshorn-Crockett', where before they could only blush. It is she who has admitted that a woman can feel loving towards a man *because* she is leaving him, and that she can get seduced by accident – not from vice or romanticism but simply by failing to spot the moment between 'I can't say no *yet*' and 'I can't say no *now*'.

Her other enormous strength, it seems to me, is detachment: the ability, while one eye is closed in a swoon, to keep the other one open, noticing. *Cast a Cold Eye* is the title of one of her books – it could be the clue title to her whole life. She has too good a head not to see what a dance her emotions are leading her – never mind, on with the dance. She observes herself and, which is a lot more dangerous, her lovers and friends; and a good deal of the venom she inspires is a result of just this. Men don't mind being denounced by a woman, but they can't stand her making a witty thing out of them. My own guess is that she is not, actually, especially malicious, even in public controversy: I get rather the impression that she says these devastating things with the immunity of a child who doesn't really believe the grown-ups can be hurt.

Quite a number of grown-ups, it must be admitted, have been sent reeling one way and another. Mary McCarthy has emotional integrity of the most disruptive kind: she says she never thinks very far ahead, and her loyalty is always to the present commitment.

It is clear from what she says that she has not married so often in a search for a never-never happiness: on the contrary. 'I'm an extremely happy person,' she said. 'Until recently I never knew what people meant when they said they were depressed.' Her recent divorce and re-marriage were not, it seems, a question of what was wrong with Bowden Broadwater but what was right with James West.

When you say that someone's new husband is an international civil servant, ex-diplomat, ex-Air Force major, who has the pink and white aspect of the conventional Senator, you tend to assume that she has simply settled down at last. But it would be a great mistake to think that, in West, Mary has found no more than a little grey home. The impulses that cause a father of three to leave a pretty housewife in her thirties for a fiftyish authoress are not standard, and nor is he. As amusing to talk to as she is, he has a Past – a cultural past, a theatre-managing past; and the force that swept Mary McCarthy off her feet was clearly the explosion of that stored charge. 'He kept saying "You remind me of the thirties",' she said; and the reawakening was symbolized for her by his books: 'His shelves were covered with books on international finance, politics, things like that; then one day they were all gone: he'd brought up his old books from the cellar and the shelves were filled with philosophy and Henry James.'

'I have this dream of us sitting in the winter by a vast stove – I'm reading Hegel, he's reading philosophy, and it's snowing outside.' Perhaps this is a mellower dream than she might have had twenty years ago; perhaps it is more realistic; but, as a romantic, she is plainly still going strong.

A romantic who can cast a cold eye on her romanticism: it is an interesting combination. I have a friend who thinks that everyone has an emotional age – not a mental age – towards which they hurry, for which they yearn. He attributes his own troubles to being emotionally eighteen, and points with amazement to management types who have apparently longed since birth to be fifty. Mary McCarthy, I should say, has a mental age of about 200 and an emotional age of twenty-four; and what novelist would ask more?

47 · *A History of Shopping*

What porridge had John Keats? is a question it becomes more and more respectable to ask; the fashion for history to concern itself with the price of tea and the varying size of collars brings it within reach, as the chain stores might say, of an increasing range of customers. And for those of us who are better at things than kings there is an excellent book out this week, *A History of Shopping*, by Dorothy Davis (Routledge).

Many of us may know something about the changes in shops since the last century, with the decline of pedlars and the rise of Mr Whiteley; but Mrs Davis is more concerned with the vast slow changes that happened before that. She writes about the medieval situation, where nothing was bought except in open markets, wholesaling was a crime that put you in the stocks, weights and measures varied from village to village and there were never enough coins – even bad ones – to go round. And she shows how all this evolved towards the nineteenth century, with far more goods bought in shops, shopkeepers generally selling rather than making their wares, and enough people buying something other than food and fuel to make mass marketing a reality.

It is odd to realize that nobody went in for fixed prices much before the late eighteenth century and I was staggered to learn that for centuries ordinary working people – in the south at least – *never* bought any but second-hand clothing; clothes 'lasted a long time, their lives seldom shortened by washing. A pair of leather stays, a double quilted horsehair petticoat, a stuff gown and a linen shift would keep the wearer

190

and her fleas warm for several years before they rotted away'.

A lot of deep prejudices get a sock in the eye from this fascinating book. Battery fowls aren't new – seventeenth-century city poulterers had turkeys in rows recovering from the long walk from Norfolk; nor are the cows that never see the clouds – nineteenth-century city folk got milk from a cow-keeper, the kept cow lowering darkly from the back shop or the cellar. Doorstep salesmen aren't just a twentieth-century plague, either: a witness giving evidence in 1833 talks of travelling Scotsmen who supplied clothes and then collected a weekly amount – 'their goods very much dearer than those from the shops . . . the lowest percentage they put on is fifty per cent and some go as high as 100 per cent'.

In fact the whole question of credit is illuminating: the Middle Ages gave everybody credit for months on end, but by the nineteenth century poor customers in debt were almost enslaved to the shops, forced to take ever shorter measure for ever higher prices. The great households, on the other hand, let their bills run for months or years. It is odd, when you consider the historical background, that it is not the poorer classes who eschew the never-never, but the richer classes, who you'd have thought were used to it.

Our image of the 'traditional' trade, nowadays, is generally of a gentleman in a frock coat crawling across a thick carpet to lick the bespoke boots of a lord; one is brought up abruptly by the realization that this was only a tiny proportion of trade generally. Shopping was more likely to have you haggling in the rain over goods sold unmeasured and unwrapped, biting your filthy change to be sure it was genuine, and nervously hoping there would not be too much alum in the flour.

Even the country markets, picturesque enough for a ballet, bore more resemblance to the screaming chaos of an eastern street market today than to the ordered country fairs now frequented by the Archers. In those days, you *had* to be tough and shrewd, without merchandise marks protection, pure food and drug Acts, or even standard weights and measures. One certainly forgets how agreeable it is not to have to buy meat where the butcher kills it, and where no one quite knew what to do with the blood and offal: Stinking Lane, Mrs Davis says, was re-christened Butchers Hall Lane 'just before Shakespeareans had a chance to point out that a road by any other name would smell of meat'.

Well, it all changed; better preservation streamlined the food trades, mass production and mass demand made chain stores a possibility; some tradesmen like Sir Thomas Lipton even rose to go yachting with royalty ('The King,' said a disgruntled German Prince, 'has gone boating with his grocer'). At the moment we do exceptionally well, poised as we are between two systems, the small and the streamlined, and getting the best of both.

Mrs Davis is no croaking raven; she is simply fascinated, as generations of shoppers were, with the details and opportunities of shopping. But the main impression the book leaves on me is that in spite of salesgirls who ignore us, cheese sweating behind its polythene, early closing days, and washing machines that consume their own nuts and bolts, we as consumers have never had it so soft.

So it seems a bit strange that it is *now* that ye olde consumer is suddenly rampant, setting up under his own sign, buttressed by testing and societies and magazines – *Focus*, a new magazine of the Consumer Council, came out a fortnight ago; there was another Bill in the consumers' interest last Thursday.

Yet maybe it is not so odd. Plenty of things become articulate only in their final stage, just as a disease can break out in visible spots after the fever has done its work; consumer organizations can take exception to this and that just because they are exceptions. After reading this book, the consumer movement seems not so much the beginning of a new dawn, as the last, explicit, final recognition that fings, fank heaven, ain't wot they used to be.

48 · In Defence of Excess

A man I know is planning to hire an aeroplane, fill it with six friends and fly to the other side of France for dinner at a restaurant which has four Michelin stars; the wines will be the best they have; he reckons it will cost him over four hundred pounds. As he is what Prince Philip would call a working journalist several of the six friends have tried to talk him out of it, urging that for the same money he could take them all to Brittany half a dozen times and have a very decent meal there.

'But if I do it this way,' he says, 'they will remember it for the rest of their lives.'

He is dead right, of course. To be memorable, it is no use being moderate. Yet all one's upbringing is in the direction of moderation. From the date of one's first party when, for fear of being sick on the carpet, one is urged to go easy on the ice-cream, we are told to be reasonable, to calm down, to see both sides of the question, to reject jobs in which the only alternatives are success or failure, and go instead for careers where a moderate success is likely enough. The process, designated by some as growing up, is described by Wordsworth as the world's slow stain; others call it coming to terms with life. Those who listen succeed from the start and go to work for advertising agencies. Yet the ones who really hit the top are the fools who work night and day at crackpot ideas, who are a trial to their wives and a burden to their families, who exasperate their employers and weary their friends – until they end up as Epstein or Maria Callas or D. H. Lawrence. Nothing succeeds like excess.

Shaw said that unreasonable men try to change the world, reasonable men change themselves to fit the world – and so it is only the unreasonable men who ever get anything done. Reasonableness and moderation are both words which could be used to describe that creeping disease whose prevalence keeps American sociologists awake at nights: the desire to be like the others, to be adjusted, to avoid extremes, to be one of the group. It is typified by the terrifying story in *The Lonely Crowd* of the mother whose son showed a keenness for the violin; she made him take extra athletics and less music: 'I want him', she said, 'to be normal.' It is rather fortunate that Mozart's family took a different line.

Anyone who suggests that most of the world's best ideas, best symphonies, best paintings have been produced by men who, if not strictly crazy, were at least tricky, fanatical, inconvenient characters, is usually confronted with the Greek ideal of moderation. But in fact the Greeks were a most immoderate lot: they were constantly fighting civil wars, slitting each other's throats, sacrificing all for nothing. Anyone who would sit for five hours on a stone seat must have been immoderately fond of tragedy; anyone who fought as they did at Thermopylæ must have been immoderately committed to the military ethic; anyone who, like Socrates, would irritate his jury into sentencing him to death must have been immoderately fond of his mission as gadfly. No doubt the Greeks thought wistfully that moderation might be a restful alternative to their way of life; but it was as much a piece of wishful thinking on their part as the British belief that the Greeks were really Old Rugbeians and great Christian gentlemen at heart.

There are, however, plenty of people who will agree that excessive enthusiasm is useful for producing the Parthenon and the Prelude, and still maintain that for the ordinary purposes of living excess is a mistake. But in fact this is not so. In the two fields which dominate the lives of almost everyone – love and money – moderation is equally disastrous.

The average moderate British male, who does not mind sandwiching a kiss or two in between the beer and the golf, is constantly surprised and irritated by the undeserved success of immoderate foreigners – men who will send a woman enormous bouquets, ring her up in the middle of the night, even (oh I *say*) burst into tears for love of her. They ought never, in the eyes of sensible men, to get anywhere at all; and yet they constantly get to home base simply because nothing charms a woman more than being loved to excess. No doubt the immoderate foreigners set their alarms to tell a woman they can't sleep for love of her; possibly a bill for the flowers will be presented in the end; but meantime the woman will be walking on air.

Conversely, the men who think they do not want to be loved to excess are usually deluding themselves. They think they do not want protestations of affection, tears when they go away and scenes when they stay away. But any man who expects (and most of them do) that a woman should constantly cook and wash and clean for him without ever being thanked or praised for it; that she should be content to sit evening after evening while he snores over the newspaper, or be told to save on hats while he smokes the price of a hat every week, or be 'understanding' if he has expense-account lunches with beautiful contacts or spends their wedding anniversary playing golf, is expecting to be loved beyond the limit of all reason or sense.

Nowhere is moderation more useless than in the manipulation of money. It is a constant wonder to journalists, actors, tramps and other go-getters that people with steady jobs always seem to have, relatively, so little to show for their large regular salaries. Such *débrouillards* do not realize that it is the very regularity of the intake which prevents anything interesting being done with the money. As Parkinson has pointed out, a small rise in salary is never actually felt at all; because expenditure simply rises imperceptibly to meet income, *and rises equally on all fronts.* It is this even distribution of expenditure which pins a man to his income group like a frog pinned to a board: he can afford the best in nothing if he buys good quality products all round – unless he is a millionaire, in which case he will lose all taste of quality altogether, having lost all sense of contrast. The man with a moderately expensive house, a wife moderately well dressed, a house moderately well furnished – even, as the eighteenth-century poet put it, 'a mistress moderately fair' has no room to manoeuvre and no feeling of being prosperous at all. Another man earning the same amount who spends half a year's salary on one superb painting, or a couple who sink the entire bank account in a sailing boat, or a family who make do with fifteen-year-old curtains to buy feed for the horses, or fifteen-year-old horses to go to the opera every night: these people are getting something positive for their money, they are doing it consciously and the fact that they may be poorer in other ways only makes them more aware of the fascinating discrepancies which life has to offer.

People who are rich and poor by turns are, as consumers, James Bond one day and St Francis the next. Their last sixpences roll around in pigskin purses; they know how it feels to tip a man – and how it feels to hope he will drop his cigar-end in their direction. The men who appreciate champagne the most are the men who drank water the night before.

There are two inestimable advantages of such up-and-down living. One is that you really appreciate luxury in all its aspects when it does come your way: you notice how pleasant it is to have a bell-hop carry your bag as well as the size of the hotel room, the cleanness of the tablecloth as well as the quality of the food. And the other is that you do not forget how it *feels* to be poor – so you do not make the mistake of thinking that the poor are all surly, undeserving and, in any case, insignificant.

Sir John Rothenstein, making the year's silliest remark, said that he had never been poor enough to own a television set – a particularly waspish expression of a well-known middle-class feeling: that what used to be called the working classes are *cheating* when they find the money for TV. From this the middle classes conclude that the poor are a lot richer than they are; but in fact all that is happening is that the 'working classes' are putting all their eggs in one basket, and refusing to pay that extra twopence here and tenpence there which goes with shopping in a 'better' neighbourhood. It is an example of mass shrewdness which should be an inspiration to us all.

Actually, of course, the middle classes have their own immoderate expenditure: the public schools. Appreciating that privileged education is worth more in the middle of the twentieth century than a decorative background or a large taxable income, they buy cardigans instead of central heating, golf clubs instead of trips to the Mediterranean, and persevere with all the austerities of British food to pay for their sons' education; and very right and proper too.

Whether you spend or love immoderately is really your own affair; in the sphere of morals, politics, and religion excess and moderation become a matter of public concern. In religion, it is generally accepted that a certain amount of enthusiasm (I use the word in its eighteenth-century sense) is permitted in the early days: Christianity without the saints, the martyrs and a P.R.O. like St Paul would never have won over the public in the way it did. But martyrs make inconvenient companions; they argue till the veins stand out

198

like knotted scourges on their foreheads; they talk one into selling all one has and giving to the poor; the thing is made to exceed all reasonable bounds. It is hardly surprising that over the years the moderates have managed to do away with that sort of thing and establish the kind of Christianity that does not, as the man said, interfere with a man's private life. It seems curst and old-fashioned to suggest that this process is just possibly deplorable: that a religion, a political theory even, might in its early, uncongenial, unmodified state perhaps be a sight more use than the conventional adaptations. Excessive Christianity, excessive liberalism, excessive anger that more than half the world's population are short of food the entire time – all these things might just possibly alter something or achieve something. But that, moderation will always prevent. Moderation is the means used by every reactionary government since politics began to draw the teeth of any reform which seriously threatened to affect the *status quo*: the reactionary party has simply brought in the measure itself, in a form designed to remove the glaring scandal without removing the basic injustice. Moderation, too, is what we all practise in the way of private charity: a half-crown in the collecting box, the occasional cheque, maybe a sale of work: nothing unreasonable. It is a good thing for us that there are one or two immoderate people who actually give up other jobs, bother to take the training and the bad pay and the anti-typhoid injections and go out and spend the money for us; the bandages and tinned food would be precious little use sitting in a warehouse – which is where they would be if a few people were not sufficiently lacerated by things like refugee camps and leper colonies actually to go out there and do something.

Even in minor, more personal ways, it is not the moderates one turns to in a fix. We all have two types of friends: the ones on whose doorstep you can turn up filthy, jobless, and in